SWEAT

by

Elizabeth-Anne Wheal

Sweat

ISBN 978-1-8380433-1-5

This edition published December 2020
Also available in paperback

ABOUT THE AUTHOR

Elizabeth-Anne Wheal is a television writer and historian. Her considerable output includes books on both world wars and an encyclopaedia of environmental issues, as well as more than seventy-five scripts for some of the UK's best-loved television dramas. She grew up in London and the US, and now lives in Norwich.

This book is dedicated to the memory of two very special women. The first is my paternal grandmother, Phyllis Beatrice Wheal – Nana – who died just before the millennium. The second is my niece, Anna Beatrice Crossman, who died suddenly, three weeks before her twenty-first birthday. Laughing off life's ups and downs – and generously helping others to laugh too – was one of the many great qualities that came very naturally to both of them, and part of my motivation in writing the book had been to share my experiences with Anna B and to enlist her help in 'seeing the funny side' as my Nana always called it. So this is for you, my beloved girl. Go figure…

June, 2020

50% of proceeds from the sale of this book will go to

ACT

THE ANNA CROSSMAN TRUST
FOR KIDS IN KERALA.

This book is dedicated to the memory of two very special women. The first is my paternal grandmother, Phyllis Beatrice Wheal – Nana – who died just before the millennium. The second is my niece, Anna Beatrice Crossman, who died suddenly, three weeks before her twenty-first birthday. Laughing off life's ups and downs – and generously helping others to laugh too – was one of the many great qualities that came very naturally to both of them, and part of my motivation in writing the book had been to share my experiences with Anna B and to enlist her help in 'seeing the funny side' as my Nana always called it. So this is for you, my beloved girl. Go figure...

June, 2020

50% of proceeds from the sale of this book will go to

ACT

THE ANNA CROSSMAN TRUST
FOR KIDS IN KERALA.

1. LIBERTY (NOVEMBER)

It started with a kiss…

Actually, that's not strictly true, but I've recently developed this habit of time-slipping into chapters from my personal Book of Life, and I was remembering Day One of Womanhood, when my first, full-on period started and I thought I'd fallen in love all on the same day. I was thirteen, on my first ever foreign holiday, on the Costa del Sol, with my twin sister, my Dad and my first stepmother, and it was hot enough to weld my flipflops to the tarmac on the road by the beach. I'd pleaded with my Dad to be allowed a moonlit walk along the water's edge with this knee-wobblingly buff, Californian teenager I'd met called Brad. He was tall as a tree, with Hollywood blond hair, topaz blue eyes, perfect white teeth and the most amazing Adam's apple I'd ever seen – a mobile, manly jewel set in a supple, sun-tanned neck – and I knew that sometime during that walk, he'd lean over me, pull me to him, and I'd be on for my first ever French Kiss…

In point of fact, though, *it* started in the Ladies' in White City Westfield, after a shopping 'therapy' episode – girls' code for wantonly buying stuff that you really don't need but you *really do* want, ignoring the fact that it's galactically overpriced.

Anyway, I'd just been into Max Mara and bought this uber-cher, off-the-shoulder cashmere top and a merely expensive pair of trousers to go with it, and I was in the Ladies', having a pee and rehearsing all the convincing things I'd say to S (my partner) when I got home about the item's real platinum thread detail and bang-for-buck exclusivity to price ratio. And I was annoyed at myself for needing to justify spending the money to him (because he only spends about £5 a year on clothes) but still keen to avoid an argument about how many months' council tax it cost. Then the solution occurred to me. Put it on now. Wear it home. That way he probably won't notice it's new, and even if he does, he's so easily seduced by the sight of my bare shoulders that I've got a good chance of deflecting any financial concerns he might have. It's a cheap strategy, but more or less guaranteed to solve the problem.

Or not. In the cramped confines of the cubicle, I've stripped down to my bra, slipped into the second most expensive cashmere top in Westfield, stuffed the shirt and jacket I was wearing into the bag, come out of the cubicle, washed my hands, and then... well, I feel hot. Not just warm, or ordinary hot, either. A boiling surge, starting low and deep, is rushing up my torso, overwhelming my upper body, face and neck. Within seconds I'm feeling sweaty and breathless and suffocated, like I've just swallowed a hot water bottle and it won't go down. I look in the mirror, relieved to note that despite swallowing a hot water bottle, my face doesn't even look red. Odd. I'm still surprised and hot and frowning back at myself in the mirror when I notice a greasy film of sweat appearing round my nose, mouth and chin, as if I've been stuffing chips with the enthusiasm of a Guinness Book of World Records chip-eating contender. I splash my face with water, which promptly drips onto the uber-cher top. I grab some toilet paper from the cubicle to wipe it dry and manage to catch a few soggy little slubs in the platinum thread detail. Shit.

A hefty squall of annoyance blows through me. I take a few breaths, tell myself it's not the end of the world, then pick out the paper slubs. While I'm doing that, I'm wondering if the heat thing is a symptom of missing eating all day. Or because I hadn't slept well the night before, unusual for me. Or because I'm pre-menstrual, except it's the wrong time of the month. Now I remember I'd felt stressed about work all day yesterday, for no obvious reason – a mood I thought I'd thrown off by self-medicating with most of a bottle of fizzy wine and several hours of TV-surfing the best of the worst reality shows. Maybe I'm going down with a cold.

But while I'm thinking this, what's concerning me more is that my armpits are clammy, which means I'm sweating onto the new top, which means I'll have to get it cleaned before I can even wear it again, and there's a TV network drinks do I'm going to later in the week that I need to dress up for. Shit. I go back into a cubicle, pull off the top, put my shirt and jacket back on. The hot feeling subsides. My irritation only partly subsides. I grab my stuff and leave. It's only when I'm on the Central Line to Liverpool Street to catch my train home that I realise I've left my highly expensive raincoat (shopping therapy session, 12.02.17, Jarrolds department store, Norwich) on the hook on the door of the toilet cubicle. SHIT.

*

A couple of weeks later, I'm out with my mate, Maj. She's in the TV business too, but she's a documentaries producer, whereas I write scripts for drama series. Her real name's Claire, but I've been calling her Maj, your Majesty or Queen Claire of Clairitania for years. It started with a funny comment from S about how she could fend off the encroachment of a new housing development by declaring independence for her tiny-but-perfectly-formed home and garden, but the joke expanded over time into the creation of a permanent alter-ego – Maj – and the acquisition of the necessary regal accoutrements: a national anthem penned by S (that ends with a rousing "she has nice hair; she is Queen Claire!"), a royal yacht (in miniature), crown jewels (plastic), the royal seal (cuddly), and even a royal crest, complete with motto – miraculo in parvitatem – which (kind of) means small is beautiful.

The regal thing has stuck partly because Maj is queenly in so many ways – she's perfectly turned out, effortlessly gracious and graceful, cool in a crisis, comfortable in any company and always in control without seeming too obvious about it. Plus I've never ever seen her washing up. Years ago, I was honoured with an appointment as her Finance Minister, which was typically acute of her, because spending money is something I mastered early in life…

It's a blowy, blustery November Sunday, and we're out on the North Norfolk coast enjoying a lip-chapping, ear-aching walk along the beach, to offset any stray guilt we might feel about heading back to our favourite pub for lunch and a glass or two. Maj has been in Paris doing some filming and getting interviews set up for a documentary she's producing. Glamorous. Apart from the over-shopping incident and the TV drinks party, I've been stuck at my desk finishing a script under the eye of a producer so young he thinks Moshe Dayan is a type of poke bowl. But what I'm keen to discuss is what's been *happening* to me…

First of all I tell Maj about the uber-cher top. Not just the cost of it, or the hot water bottle incident in Westfield, but the naked, shameful truth of it: I just can't wear the fricking thing. Every time I put it on, even for five minutes, it makes me sweat. I'm not certain, but I'm concerned that this is some kind of disastrous, mid-life morality spread – a subconscious rejection of self-indulgence. Maj nods and looks thoughtful but says nothing for now; like the Queen she is, she's a great listener and rarely speaks in an unconsidered way.

I explain that I tried to take the sweater back to Max Mara but the snooty cow of a sales girl actually sniffed it – right there in front of me – wrinkled her nose up and said she suspected "it has been worn, Madam…". Then, while she was ostentatiously examining it, she'd noticed a micro-slub of dried toilet paper stuck to the platinum thread detail, so that was that. I admit to Maj that the offending item is now, despite its exorbitant cost, squished into the back of a cupboard, probably never to see the light of day again. Maj doesn't judge me or mention charity shops or Ebay or even flinch at this. She's great like that.

Then I tell her about the TV drinks night, for which, as I point out bitterly, I'd bought the unwearable top in the first place (only half true but anyway…). I preface my story with a good moan about winter. While Maj looks great at all times, in all seasons and over all the years I've known her, for me there's a distinct physical cliff I drop off each year, triggered by the changing of the clocks. As if by temporal-corporeal agreement, my body responds to the end of BST by simply letting go. Everything goes to crap – hair, skin, nails, weight… and holding back the collapse is complicated by a seasonal addiction to crisps and chocolate, and a parallel aversion to vegetables or fresh fruit. I dread that annual all-goes-to-hell trigger moment.

It shouldn't matter what I look like, I whine. My talent as a writer is not a function of my waist size or hair voluptuousness. But the grim truth is that in a ruthlessly 'talent-based' industry like television, appearances matter. So, as I point out to Maj, I'm already having a bad hair day as I set off for the drinks do at which I was hoping to impress, or at least get a lead on my next job.

The deal with these schmoozing parties – attended by TV management plus actors, directors, producers, writers and, normally, a small band of paparazzi – is that you turn up, tell everyone how busy you are, pretend you're all mates and not in the least bit competitive, clap everything on the 'hurray, aren't we brilliant' video of the company's latest output, network your socks off and drink fizzy wine that goes to your head and makes you feel mildly nauseous. On a good day you manage to deliver a few pitches to a few producers to tee up some job possibilities, before you find a mate and head off to a bar to swap pay-scale secrets and discuss the golden years of television (*always* involving shows you both worked on). But tonight deviates from the norm in so many ways...

I'm in the taxi approaching the Liberal Club where the party is being held, when my internal central heating clicks on. Within a minute, I've gone from cool, composed and feeling perfectly okay in my fallback

LBD and heels, to ripping off my coat, checking my armpits for deodorant stains and groping frantically in the bottom of my bag for a tissue to dry off my face and neck. I've just managed to do that without smearing my makeup too much, when I spot the gathered paparazzi jostling for position and training their lenses expectantly on the cab as it slows and stops outside the Club.

Under no illusion that I'm a celeb, I'm still a bit gutted when I push open the taxi door to step out into the rain, and the waiting paps issue what sounds to me like a communal groan of disappointment. Their cameras drop back onto their chests, and they go back to grumbling among themselves without wasting a nanosecond of digital time on me. As I totter past them up the steps to the front door, they're so thoroughly uninterested they don't even bother to check, as they have done on other occasions, that I'm not some super-powerful but so far anonymous TV executive recently arrived from the US or the Antipodes. Obviously not my night to dazzle.

Once in the room – a huge, high ceilinged, overheated expanse full of men and women in black (unofficial TV uniform) – I grab a drink and insert myself into a little gaggle of schmoozers standing around an executive producer (male, 60s) who I, and clearly others, hope to get some work from. It's hard to get a word in though, because the exec producer is being vigorously chatted-up by a startlingly-dressed 20-something actor. She's got seven-inch wedges on, making her taller than Brienne out of Game of Thrones; she's also wearing tights dramatically overprinted with the New York skyline in duplicate. My eyes (and everyone else's) are uncomfortably glued to the tips of twin Chrysler Buildings disappearing between her legs, as I exchange who-are-yous with a fellow schmoozer – a 40-something author hoping to break into telly. She blinks and nods vaguely, looking neither interested nor impressed by anything I have to say to her, then excuses herself and walks off to join her agent.

The exec is still on his unofficial tour of New York's better-known landmarks. I spot a producer friend and go over for a chat. He cheerily tells me that his girlfriend's pregnant and that he's taking a break from producing – which from my point of view is hardly good news: he won't have any work to offer me for at least a year. I'm managing to smile and congratulate him all the same, when my internal radiator kicks suddenly back into action. I try to ignore it and focus on what he's saying about BBC drama commissioning, but suddenly I'm looking through his eyes, watching my face break out in greasy globules of sweat.

I stare at him, trying to assess his reaction. He stares back with a slightly querying expression, but I can't tell if this is because of what's sprouting on my face or because I'm staring strangely at him. He's still talking but all I'm aware of is what feels like bulging beads of sweat jostling for position as they colonise my face and neck. Luckily, my friend excuses himself at this point to answer a call from his girlfriend.

As he walks away, I have a surreptitious dab at my face with my already damp tissue, but it does nothing to combat the feeling that I've just come off court after a solo five-setter against the whole Murray family. I'm telling myself not to panic when I spot a potential solution to my problem – a large, full jug of iced water – sitting on a table in one of the big, tall-windowed bays behind me. I sidle over, already anticipating the relief of a cold drink, only to discover that there are no glasses, and mine's still full of fizz. Dismissing the urge to pick up the jug in two hands and drink straight from it, or simply pour it over my head, I make a quick check for observers, turn my back to the gathering, dip the tip of my tissue into the water and then quickly wipe my face with it.

It's bliss – but only for a few seconds. I feel another surge, as if someone's just cranked up my thermostat. I recce the immediate vicinity and risk a surreptitious double dip of the water jug. As I dab at my face again, I'm hit with a panicky pang of super-self-consciousness, self-pity and simultaneous loss of purpose. What am I doing, standing here on my own clutching a soggy tissue, a woman on the verge of spontaneous combustion? Right now, TBH, I'd rather be at home doing my accounts, or cleaning hair out of the washing machine filter. Anxious thoughts lift-off with my body temperature. What if someone has spotted my strange behaviour? What if my whole career is about to plunge downhill as news reaches my colleagues that I'm having some kind of water-related mental breakdown? Sweat is now escaping my armpits in measurable amounts, I can feel it trickling down my sides and soaking into the tight waist of my dress. Yet another mini Gulf Stream of panic and heat washes over me, spiked with furious indignation. I SO don't need this! Suddenly I'm outside my body again, visualising myself as I rip off my hot, clingy LBD, throw my toe-jamming high heels through the window and tell the whole room where they can stick it before stalking out in bra and knickers. Whoa!

Determined to divert myself from any more career-trashing and possibly sectionable fantasies, I put down my wine and head towards the exit, delivering a couple of smiles to no one in particular and hoping my expression says that I've got really important calls to make or a choice of much more interesting places to be, and not just that I'm running off to hide in the loos and check myself the hell out.

I leave the room through heavy oak double doors. I'm into an expanse of thick-carpeted upper hallway that encircles the huge, ornate staircase in the middle of the building. I spot a sign for The Ladies' on the far side. I totter round in my heels, wary of them catching in the deep red, gorily patterned pile, but as I pass the head of the stairs I deviate suddenly, taking a sharp left towards them… and *away* from the Ladies.

I'm out of my body, watching myself. What the hell am I doing? It looks like I'm going for an escape. Most of me is shocked, guilty and horrified – are you *serious*? This isn't how to get your next commission, pay the bills, fulfill your professional and personal obligations – but I seem to be doing it anyway. I descend past portraits of Liberal Party glitterati through the ages: Gladstone, Asquith, Lloyd George. They stare back at me with sneering condescension: "if you can't stand the heat....". I get to the bottom of the stairs, collect my coat from the cloakroom and hurry breathlessly back out onto Whitehall Place and into the cold. At least the paps have disappeared. Another surge of sweaty guilt is relieved by the cooling effect of the rain on my face. Before the next guilt surge arrives, I spot and hail a cab, climb in, slam the door shut, and ask the back of the driver's head to take me to Liverpool Street, as fast as possible, please.

*

In the familiar, anonymous, comforting darkness of the back seat, the fight-or-flight adrenaline levels subside somewhat, and I begin a debrief with myself, along the lines of: WTF just happened? Have I got something serious wrong with me? Should I be heading straight for Accident and Emergency instead of the 8.30 from LST? Have I blown any chance of some income in the near future by copping out of the party early? As we slow to a stop for a red light, I notice that the driver has an A to Z in his hand. Unusual. A minute later, at the next red light, the driver is studying the book again. I feel buttons being pressed. Is it really *that* challenging to locate a central London transport hub used by tens of millions of people a year?!

I tsk loudly, hoping he can hear me, and then, when he seems to ignore this, I ostentatiously copy the cab's license number onto my phone, hoping he's noticed (which he hasn't, he's too busy map reading) and in case I feel that an official complaint is necessary. Then I go back to my internal debrief.

Five minutes later, I've decided that leaving the party early is no kind of disaster, and that I'm probably just over-tired – when I look up to see that we're arriving at... Hyde Park Corner?! We seem to have bounced like a well-flippered pinball off the embankment at Hungerford Bridge, and then followed a wide, arcing *reverse* trajectory round St James's and Green Park until we're more or less, but not even quite back where we started! I see red. I feel red. I throw myself forward and snap angrily through the slit in the glass dividers:

"Why are we back here? What the hell's going on?!"

The driver mumbles something in a heavy accent that includes the words, borrowed, cab, not sure, way...

"You've got to be joking! Hand me the A to Z. *I'll* tell you the way to go!"

He pushes the book sulkily through the slit. I land back in my seat with a steaming, hot hiss of annoyance, and start mentally composing my outraged email to the Black Cab Drivers' Association (or whatever) as I open the A to Z on the enlarged City pages, looking for the shortest, most efficient shortcut back to the station. I'll show *him*!

Or maybe not...

Something's wrong. I frown and blink, but I can't see the map clearly. It's out of focus. I tip the page towards the side windows to catch light from streetlamps as we pass them, but it's like trying to read under strobe lights. What's wrong with my eyes? First the heat, then the adrenaline rush, and now I can't see properly. Before I've even considered alternate courses of action, I've shoved the A to Z back through the slit, barked at the driver to stop, thrown open the door, chucked a fiver at him through the half open window and stalked off up Piccadilly.

I walk a few yards, coat clutched round me against the rain, then stop in the shelter of a chemist's shop awning, shivering with external cold and internal heat, a Baked Alaska in reverse. My heart's pounding like the train I wish I was on. I feel a bit dizzy. I need to take myself in hand. I'll get a cup of tea somewhere, then find a cabbie who can navigate a fricking cab!

As I'm about to walk on, I glance through the window of the

chemist's – one of those posh, oldy-worldy ones with apothecary's jars behind a mahogany counter covered in mud and seaweed-based beauty products, on sale at champagne prices. In the corner of the shop is a revolving rack of upmarket plastic reading glasses that they sell to old people whose sight is failing but who still want to look 'trendy'. I stop dead as my thought process takes a few, staggering steps forward. Does that explain it? Am I getting age-related vision loss? I reject the idea as quickly as I've had it. It's not possible. I'm not nearly old enough. Anyway, it wouldn't happen like that... to be able to see totally clearly one minute and not see at all the next... would it?

Back in the pub, on our second glass, I ask Maj to help me interpret these events. Why can't I wear cashmere, handle a TV drinks do, stay cool, or read in the back of a cab? She puts a hand on my arm, gently knocking a splash of rosé onto my sleeve. In her soothing, sexy but not overly husky voice, she says:

"Most people's eyesight gets a bit weaker as they get older, darling."

"I guess..." I concede reluctantly.

"But as to the wider issues, have you thought..." she hesitates. "I don't want to alarm you, but   it's possible you're

"Possible I'm what?" I interrupt nervously.

*

Maj drops me off in the city centre, next to the Forum – a large, modern, glass-fronted but otherwise underwhelming building that houses the local BBC news studio and tourist office, various food outlets, some exhibition space and the main Norwich library. I've got some revisions to finish on a script that's in pre-production, but that's suddenly taken a back seat to my much more urgent mission: I'm heading straight to the library to find something to read about *peri-menopause*. I need to nail what's going on right now, and an actual book by a real expert seems a safer bet than googling. Maj says peri-menopause is the precursor to the menopause proper, but I've never heard of it – it sounds more like a sailing manoeuvre or a grammatical rule for an obscure language.

It occurs to me that I've never given the menopause any thought, let alone a peri-version. My Mum never talked about it, and she's been dead for years so I can't ask her now. Caroline, my twin sister, has never mentioned it. We've also got a gang of mates that we've known since all-girls high school days, and it definitely hasn't featured on our WhatsApp group. My oldest, best mate Lou, who lives in San Francisco, has been having night sweats for years, but she's always put it down to her overenthusiastic consumption of Napa Valley's finest, and to her work as a location sound engineer, which requires high levels of physical exertion.

The phrase, 'Change of Life' bubbles up as I push my way through the weekend crowds of skateboarders, emos and young families hanging about on the shallow-stepped plaza in front of the Forum. My stomach flip-flops. Hold on, I think... all *that* stuff is for other women – older women... isn't it? I stop at the Library doors, pull my mobile out and call Caroline. Everything that's ever happened to me has happened to her, more or less. Being twins I guess you could say that's normal. But we share an odd kind of synchronization-cum-empathy, and we often know what's happening to each other, and when, without actually talking about it.

So, as I press 'call', I assume she'll say she was just about to phone me to discuss symptoms.

"Hi, hon, it's me. Are you busy?"

"Kind of – cooking for eight tonight... wassup?"

"Quick question. Are you getting any peri-menopause symptoms?"

"What?" I'm not sure she's entirely listening.

"Peri-menopause – apparently it's what happens before the 'change of life'. Are you getting any weird stuff happening to you?"

"Like what, hot flushes, d'you mean ...?" she says, sounding like she's more interested in rinsing her chicory or whatever it is she's doing while talking to me.

"Yeah."

"Nope."

"You're definitely not getting hot and sweaty at odd moments?"

"No."

"Disturbed nights?"

"Head hits the pillow, I'm a goner".

"Panicky? Distracted? Annoyed?"

"All of the above – but only when Guy gets out his toolbag and says he fancies a bit of weekend shelf-building." (My brother-in-law's a great bloke, and handy at DIY, but definitely one of your messier homo sapiens.)

"What about your eyes?"

"My eyes?

"Any problems?"

She chuckles down the phone. "Yeah... incredibly enough, that's why I've been wearing glasses *since we were twelve.*"

"Point..."

Pause. "Are you okay?" There's suddenly a mild note of concern in her voice.

"Yeah... no, actually... I think... I dunno... I keep getting these sweats and I'm feeling... sort of nervy and grumpy and strange... I think *it* might be starting... I might be falling off the precipice of middle age."

She laughs as if I'm joking. "Kay... well text me when you hit the bottom and I'll tell everyone to delete you out of their contacts. Gotta go, my stock's boiling over. Love ya. Byee".

I stare at the silent phone for a second. I guess for now I'm on the quest for knowledge alone.

*

The library is full of youth, mostly chatting or surfing the net rather than reading books, but I patronisingly decide that that's better than not being in the library at all – at least the kids are *in physical proximity* to books, in case they suddenly feel the urge to try one out. I head upstairs to the appropriate section and quickly spot nine or ten titles featuring the M word, including *Making Friends with the Menopause* which for some reason makes me feel a bit nauseous. *The Wisdom of Menopause*? No thanks. Another title soberly offers me *Managing Menopause*. I take it off the shelf and flick through. It's very medical. And long. I want something that tells me quickly and in layman's language whether I'm peri-menopausal or not and if so, what that means for me – preferably a very short handbook. But for some reason there doesn't seem to be anything quite like that. Annoying.

Too impatient to wait 'til I get home, I hustle a couple of teenage girls off a terminal – all they're doing is gossiping about oral sex – and sit down to google PERI-MENOPAUSE. The first few links are useless:

Peri-menopause and thrush – I decide not to go there for now.

Are you in peri-menopause? Knowing about peri-menopause can help plan ahead. Plan ahead for what?? It sounds scary, like a death sentence. I move on to:

Peri-menopause – what is it? I click on that one, but what I get is mystifying: *hormonal imbalance... a result of fluctuations in sex hormone levels... expect changes in the cycling and ratios of...* and then a list of things that sound like hormones.

Whatever. I go back to Google and click on an article in the womens' section of *The Guardian*. It's a 30-something woman's personal story of two years of hell while she thought she was dying, when in fact she was experiencing very early menopause. Two paragraphs down, courage fails me. I decide to stick with info about 'normal' menopause. Back to google for a link to 'ten common symptoms'. That's got to be the business.

But it's not.

It starts with a lengthy and chummily condescending 'poor you...' introduction, then says, *'over the following pages we will discuss...'* No! I don't want discussion or sympathy. I want information. And not too much of it either. I'm not *at all interested* in peri-menopause as such, I just want headlines. This is what to expect, this is how long it will last. End of.

I google hot flushes instead, but the description I get is inconclusive: *'hot flushes may be felt anywhere on the body but most often on the neck and face, making women feel 'hot' often accompanied by reddening of the skin.'* But I don't get actual 'reddening' at all, and 'face and neck' doesn't even begin to cover where I've started feeling hot. And what do they mean by quote-hot-quote – how is 'hot' different to unquoted hot?

I feel irritation rising. Now I can't decide whether what I had at Westfield, at the Liberal Club and a good few times since then constitute hot flushes or not. Maybe I'm getting an allergy or something. I'm about to google flushes plus allergies when I notice a youth in bum-slung board shorts and a baseball cap staring uncompromisingly at the screen over my shoulder while he waits for a terminal to come free. Embarrassed and suddenly extremely annoyed by this spotty, gormless, fashion-victim nobody's attack on my space and my privacy, I quit the browser with a rap of the keys, push my chair back so violently I bang into his leg, get up, mumble something that doesn't sound too convincing as an apology, and leave.

As I head down the stairs, I'm a bit shocked to notice the Library first-aider arriving to treat a small but copiously bleeding gash on Gormless but now very surprised-looking Boy's shinbone. And I don't even *really* feel all that guilty about it. Weird.

I head home to the privacy of my own laptop. With another churning tumble in the pit of my stomach, I fully confront the possibility that Maj is right – that I might be arriving at that 'gateway moment' – when I go from being normal, female me to being… what? Someone else? I get a sudden rush of regret and imminent loss. Is that it for the me that's existed up til now? Am I going to lose my me-ness without even having thought about it? And if so, who or what is me going to become now? I haven't got a clue. Normally, I pride myself on planning. I'm good at anticipating problems and strategising solutions. But this is something I've utterly failed to prepare for. I can't believe that I've let something *this* momentous catch me unrehearsed. How could this have happened? Am I losing the plot?

Related questions jostle for first place in my consciousness.

Will the menopause involve pain or other physical suffering? Will I suddenly adopt a different attitude to ads for funeral plans, anyone in a hoody and the really dark stuff on TV? Is it inevitable that my pubes will now go grey and wiry, and my tits will deflate, leaving me with a chest that looks like it's got two empty icing bags stuck to it? Why am I thinking in such a negative, image-based way about this anyway? What's so important and defining about my body dumping a bucketful of blood every month? What's significant *at all* about remaining fertile beyond 50? And while I'm asking, why did Gormless Boy make me so annoyed, so quickly, that causing him bodily harm felt almost… righteous?

I close my laptop. It's time to deliver a sobering heads up to S, who's in the kitchen, descaling the coffee machine and reading a book about England's Sailing Navy. I'm waiting for his mouth to drop open as I reveal that, in the not too distant future, The Menopause may be docking round our way for a prolonged stay in port – but instead he shrugs and grins, points out the upside of contraceptive-free sex, and suggests that when and as it drops anchor, we could approach The Change as the start of another phase in the grand adventure that is our life together.

Normally, I appreciate S's jokey spin on almost any situation. But for some reason, his levity makes me want to pick up the coffee machine and drop it on his foot.

***

2. DOCTOR, DOCTOR (DECEMBER)

I should be pulling up my big pants and getting on with life, aka work, aka earning. Money seems to be haemorrhaging out of our accounts, mostly for items with a below-zero feel-good rating – like appliance insurance – and I still haven't succeeded in nailing my next job. *And* it's Christmas. S is busy editing harrowing reports about slave labour for a global NGO, but the bottom line is that, worthy and highly sensitive work though this is, it doesn't command all that much in the way of a fee. When he's not editing reports, he's writing history books and the odd short story, but they don't earn much either and it's my work that largely pays the bills. All I've got for now, though, is an invitation to present 'some ideas' for an episode of a popular murder mystery series that I've written for in the past. And that means it could be months before anyone starts talking about writing me an actual cheque.

Normally, this wouldn't concern me. I'd be glued to my desk, totally focused on conjuring up larger-than-life characters and weaving murderous motivations into the high gloss set-ups favoured by the programme. But I'm not. I'm distracted and edgy. I'm asking myself why women I know don't ever talk about the M word. Why the big silence? And more broadly, how come I can't turn to my favourite book or play or Aretha Franklin classic for insights? Why doesn't it turn up on my newsfeed? And if you look at literature, where are all the menopausal women? Lady Macbeth? Now I come to think about it, early menopause might explain quite a lot about her...

I've *got* to concentrate, but it's getting harder ever since I put myself on emergency self-observation detail: am I feeling odd/different/

unwell? Can I read that font size as easily as I could yesterday? And although none of the sites I've found so far has been at all satisfactory, I keep going back to the net to symptom-search. I'm thinking I really should go and talk to a doctor. Because some pretty strange things *are* happening.

I'm getting bad headaches – a first for me – and my heart feels poundy quite a lot of the time, even when I'm not consciously worrying about anything. In fact I've recently noticed that I can hear my heart-beat pounding in my ears when I get into bed every night. S thinks this is because we've just had the window replaced, so the previously pre-sent ear-pounding isn't drowned out by street noise any more, but that doesn't convince me at all. I'm feeling tired quite a lot of the time. And I've noticed myself reacting oddly to things, and spiking 0 to 60 anxiety over little ishoos that wouldn't normally even make it into my ishoo in-tray. I seem to need to pee more often. And hot water bottle episodes are just the half of it, literally.

I've started experiencing a sort of inversion effect: first I feel the heat firing up and radiating through me, followed by cartoon levels of upper body sweating; then, as the sweating cools me down, I start to feel cold, or even freezing cold. As a result, infuriatingly, I'm having to change my whole approach to what I wear. Despite the weather being arctic, I'm having to avoid anything thick, anything made of wool or woolly fabric; anything with a neck; anything with a lot of man-made fibres in it; anything that's too tight or clingy, especially from my waist up. And even then, I'm finding I have to keep taking stuff off and putting it on again every two minutes. It's embarrassing. I've noticed the odd customer watching me in cafés as I huff in and out of my jacket five times in ten minutes.

I've also had two bleeds in one month, and they're definitely periods nouveaux. I used to have 'normal' five or six day downloads, accompanied by low to medium level pain in most of my lower half –

not too bad, really, considering what some women I know go through every month. But now, in the space of twelve hours, I bloat up like an over-breakfasted python, then my body expels the total contents of my uterus in a screamingly painful, forty-eight-hour bloodbath version of that bloke in Alien giving birth to one. And while that's happening, I feel really ill, like I'm going down with flu.

I'm a bit washed out as a result. I feel the need to keep a towel permanently on emergency duty in the car and carry half of Superdrug's stock of 'feminine essentials' everywhere I go, just in case. I'm also being forced to apply a new set of criteria to upcoming social and work commitments. Yesterday I said no to going on location in the Oxfordshire countryside to watch a script being filmed, because it sounded like I might get stranded too far away from decent toilet facilities.

On top of this, my nights aren't so much disturbed any more as fundamentally re-routined. Sometimes I wake up every fifteen minutes for no apparent reason. Sometimes I lie there for a couple of minutes, wondering why I've woken up, before a tsunami of sweat floods over my body, necessitating a miserable trip to a cold bathroom to towel myself dry, or even shower. Or… I wake up, having thrown off all the bedclothes in a wild, dream-filled sweat, freezing and shivering and scrabbling to cover myself up. Or… I wake up and nothing happens. And then I can't get back to sleep for thinking it will.

Plus there are the viral lists. In the past, when I haven't been able to sleep because something serious/scary/important is happening, I've made mental to-do lists of possible solutions, as a way of reassuring myself back to sleep. But now, once I've started listing, I really can't stop. These lists include everything, from important stuff like doing my tax return, to marginally less crucial items such as whether I've run out of vegetable stock pots, but it's as if I've regressed mentally, and can no longer differentiate, triage or prioritise, so that *everything* feels equally urgent.

S is occasionally insomniac, so he's accustomed to thrashing about at night, getting up again to stare at the test match, or watch the clock tick past five or six in the morning. But I'm used to going to sleep instantly and waking up about seven hours later, feeling smugly well-rested and having hardly moved an inch, so this new routine is exhausting as well as troubling.

I'm also developing a problem with physical proximity. Me and S have always had a happily physical relationship, but that's getting less and less feasible by the minute. These days, I can only stand our bodies coming into contact in any meaningful way for about fifteen seconds before I wriggle away, feeling hot and sticky, mildly claustrophobic and more than a bit sorry for myself. As a result, I'm starting to feel *physically* detached – from S, from myself even.

I guess this *could* all be down to a peri-menopausal crisis I'm suffering. But if peri-menopause is this bad, surely *someone* would have warned me about it before now? Hot flushes and maybe tiredness I'd heard of, but no one's ever mentioned physical and emotional meltdown as part of the deal. So *what if it isn't peri-menopause*? What if I've actually got something *serious* wrong with me, and I'm busy putting all the symptoms down to The Change. All of a sudden this makes horrible sense.

I've always prided myself on never going to the doctor. It's a particularly British thing, obviously – enduring pain and illness beyond reason, and thinking that makes you a better person. Maybe it's an unintended consequence of having a free-at-the-point-of-delivery health service. It's there if you really need it, so you try and tough it out. And anyway, doctors are still pretty good at making you feel guilty for even setting foot in their surgery/hospital, unless you're missing body parts, or dragging round a tumour the size of a butternut squash. So you end up being brainwashed into the idea that decent people just don't go.

In any case, today is the day that my stiff upper lip is making a permanent exit, along with my temperature control and any lingering delusion I had about immortality. I've decided to seek expert help for my concerns. I've also decided not to wait for an appointment with my own doctor, who is a tall, lean, attractive Scotsman of about 50. He's intelligent, down-to-earth, with a reassuring, dry sense of humour, but as a result of all these attributes he's incredibly popular with patients, so seeing him always means a wait. Instead, I'm going for a see-some-one-the-next-day appointment with one of the female doctors that I've never met before. Better though, really, I tell myself. She's female, so she'll empathise, even if she's younger than me. She'll *get* how I'm feeling and what I'm talking about...

I'm having a bit of a heat rush as I walk into her room, so I get out a tissue (I've started buying those little 'handy travel' packets that always seemed so pointless before, and making sure I've got a few with me at all times). I settle in the chair opposite her. She's in her early 40s, I reckon. I smile ruefully and say I'm feeling a bit hot. She doesn't react. Not even a smile. She calls up my notes on her screen and swivels slightly towards me in her chair.

"How can I help, today?"

She wants to help. Good. I begin. I tell her about the headaches, the wakefulness, the peeing, the pounding heart, the hot and cold rushes, the anxiety, the lists and the tidal periods. She listens, features impassive. I imagine hopefully that she's deep in contemplation of my problems, calculating things I don't understand, and making fine judgements as she absorbs all this. Finally, I get through the list and wonder out loud, slightly self-consciously, whether these all might be symptoms of peri-menopause.

"Hmmm," she says. While I wonder how to interpret her hum, she takes my pulse, then pulls out the blood pressure machine. I watch as she wraps the blow-up collar round my arm, pumps it up and stares at the read-out. I assume she's still contemplating and calculating.

"How is it?" I ask as she unwraps the blow-up collar again.

"Within normal limits," she says almost grudgingly. I'm about to ask why she didn't just say 'normal', when:

"Do you smoke?"

Here we go.

"Yes," I say, watching her closely to judge her response. Impassive reboots as unmistakably disapproving. I've dropped crucial empathy points.

"How many a day?" She's turned back to her screen now and she's rapidly keying in figures and stuff, as if she's already given up on me as a person and is happier to deal with me as a set of notes and numbers.

"Minimum one, maximum, five."

"How long for?"

"Oh... since I was..." I try and offer a balanced lie. "Sixteen?"

She keys more figures in.

"You really need to stop."

"I know. I've cut down". This cuts no ice. It's not true anyway.

"Once you're into your fifties you become much more susceptible to a whole range of smoking related diseases, you know."

What I really want to say at this point is: 'Do you think I've been living under a radio-wave-suppressing duvet in Diego Garcia for my WHOLE life? OF COURSE I KNOW!!!!!! I could hardly have missed the cadaverous faces on NHS cancer videos, or the goo pouring out of compromised arteries in 'what this does to your heart' adverts, or that scary picture of the witchy female smoker wearing canyons of flesh instead of a face, that used to turn up all the time on Facebook...'. But all I actually say is:

"Yes".

"We run a quit smoking clinic here on Mondays and Thursdays."

"I've seen the posters..."

"What's your weight and height?"

I provide her with those details.

"Cholesterol count?"

"It was checked a couple of months ago…"

She scrolls down my notes. "Ah, yes."

More keying-in.

"We have a new software program. It can tell us about your risk of heart disease."

"Oh".

We seem to have veered right off the path of my info-quest. The doc swivels back round towards me with a mild air of 'ta-da!'

"According to the program", she explains curtly, "you have an eleven and a half percent risk of having a heart attack."

I frown. That doesn't sound *too* bad… but… "Eleven and a half percent in relation to...?"

"In relation to nothing. That's your percentage risk. At twenty percent we put you on statins. It would go down to..." She keys in more figures. "...eight and half percent if you didn't smoke".

"Doesn't sound like a *huge* difference."

"Hmmmm."

"So as far as the sweating and the headaches are concerned…" I say… but now she's turned away again and she's filling in an online field and saying:

"We'll take some blood, run a few tests – thyroid, kidney and liver function – you can call for the results in a couple of weeks, then we'll see where we go from there."

She smiles briefly but without warmth as she gives me a form. "Hand that to reception as you leave."

*

On the way home, I berate myself: why did I meekly walk out without pressing her on whether my symptoms were all peri-menopausal, or if not, what she thinks might be wrong? I'm annoyed that she didn't seem that interested either way. And I'm confused, too. Why on earth wouldn't she have made it clear to me, if my symptoms *were* likely to be menopausal? Was it because she didn't think they were? In which case, I was right – I *have got something else wrong with me*. Eleven and a half percent risk of a heart attack is now sounding a lot bigger than it did in the surgery. It's more than one in ten. I look into the faces of the people I pass in the street as I march home to the rhythm of my raised heartbeat. What percentage risk have they got? It occurs to me suddenly that my father and grandfather both died from heart disease and my mother had what might have been a heart attack when she was in her early sixties.

Come to think of it, she also had an overactive thyroid when me and my sister were young. I remember this with a jolt that stops me in my tracks, and causes the young mother behind me to rake my ankles with the wheels of her child's travel system (previously known as a pushchair or buggy). She doesn't apologise, because she's a young mother with a travel system and they own the Universe (along with most supermarket aisles, lifts, airport departure lounge queues and all the standing room in buses, at all times, everywhere).

Memories of my mum In The Time of Thyroid swipe in front of my eyes as I walk on. One day she was herself – easygoing, well-organised and happy. Then seemingly the next she was permanently overheated and sweaty, ridiculously thin, utterly intolerant and very angry and anxious about almost everything. She got headaches. She shouted at total strangers. Her eyes went boggly. Then they sent her for surgery, which involved slitting her neck open from one side to the other, and closing it up afterwards, not with stitches but with tiny, metal bulldog clips. I remember my boyfriend of the time driving me and Caroline to the hospital in his Rover 2000 to collect her. On the way home we went over a bump, my Mum's head snapped back, two of the bulldog clips popped off and we all screamed.

Back home, I know I probably shouldn't, but I google overactive thyroid. NHS UK tells me that hyper-thyroidism's symptoms include: hyperactivity; mood swings; insomnia; fatigue; muscle weakness; weight loss; needing to go to the bathroom more; excess sweating; loss of interest in sex. OMG. Mood swings, check. Fatigue, check. Difficulty sleeping, check. Sweating, check. Peeing more often, check. Hyperactivity, check (that's feeling restless, right?). Weight loss, check (well I'd lost a pound last time I went on the scales). Loss of interest in sex, check – I can't stay close enough to S to *get* interested let alone stay that way. I hit the tab marked 'complications' and read on: undiagnosed or poorly controlled overactive thyroid can lead to a rare but serious reaction called THYROID STORM. It affects roughly 1 in 100 people with hyper-thyroidism. A thyroid storm is a medical emergency if...

I burst into S's office upstairs to get him up to speed. He's still focusing on Burmese slave labour as I reel off my symptoms and describe the likely, indeed the probable emergency-in-waiting. If I don't get this across now, he won't know how to react when the thyroid storm explodes inside me and I'll die before he's even thought to ring 999!

He makes a throwaway comment over his shoulder about overactive imaginations as I continue my panic briefing. I can't decide whether to just ignore his insensitivity or to spin him round violently in his typing chair, drive biros through his hands and demand his full attention to the fact that I'm quite possibly going to die BEFORE HIS VERY EYES! In the end, though, I just huff in a 'you obviously don't care if I live or die' way, leave him to it and go and call my sister.

I tell her I think I might have an overactive thyroid, like our mum. She tells me to go straight on Skype so she can examine my eyes and see if they're starting to boggle. This turns out to be a bad idea. As I stretch my neck and lean towards the camera eye in my laptop so she can get a close up, she says:

"What's that lump?"

"What lump?"

"There, kind of under your jaw at the top of your neck, on the side."

*

Now I've seen and felt the lump, it's huge, uncomfortable and quite obviously malignant (one of the ugliest words in the English language, I've always thought). I've made *another* appointment at the doc's for tomorrow and I'm trying to stay calm about having to wait a whole day for diagnosis by switching my focus to Christmas. S is a Christmas denier because he's implacably committed to the truth about the whole festival: that it is, in fact, a ruthless, commercially-constructed trap, mostly invented by American marketeers of the early twentieth century, whose sole purpose is to skin us for exponentially bigger sums of cash than they can get away with for the rest of the year. So normally, while I'm getting cheerfully fleeced for stuff to share with friends and family, the best I can hope for from S is that he'll keep smiling about the transformation of the house, the filling of the fridge and the emptying of our bank account.

But this year's different. This year, even *my* Christmas is being invaded by doubt. I've amassed a lot of lists – my first line of defence in any event management situation – but somehow I don't seem to be ticking things off. I've started writing cards, but I haven't finished them. I've ordered some beef for Christmas dinner, but I've still got to decide on food for the other days. And I'm behind with presents. I'm not experiencing any Christmas sparkle. And it's making me feel edgy – and a bit useless.

I walk down to John Lewis, only to discover that shopping as such is impossible, because ten people per square metre are milling round every doorway, display, escalator and till. So I head off to The Lanes, a grid of attractive cobbled streets where Norwich's small, independent shops, bars and restos cluster for mutual support against the encroaching chain stores. But while I'm staring at displays of pretty things in a jeweller's shop window, I'm running a non-stop (and increasingly maddening) dialogue with myself about whether all this is relevant if I'm going to die from The Lump, and how much stuff I've still got to do if I'm not. I give up and go home.

Maj, just back from a whirlwind work trip to Montreal, is standing on my front steps, resplendent in pink-cheeked health and a cool new coat and hat, as I plough up the path, muttering to myself.

"Hello, darling - am I early?"

"Earlier the better, Maj. I may have limited time left." I fumble miserably in my bag for my keys as she hugs me soothingly.

"You know there are hundreds of things that lump could be that aren't cancer."

I feel a glimmer of reassurance. Somehow if Maj says something, I believe it could be true.

Back at the surgery the next day to see the doctor (another female stranger) I show her the lump. She pushes at it. She feels the other side of my neck.

"I don't think it's a gland or swelling."

"Not a tumour, then, or my thyroid...."

She doesn't respond to this either way. "I think it's your transverse process," she says.

"What's that?"

She turns to a picture of the human skeleton on her wall and points. "It's that bone there."

There is indeed a small bone that sticks out either side of the spine, right at the top.

"But I couldn't feel it like this before. It never used to stick out like that."

She doesn't offer an explanation as to why it should now. She just smiles in a kindly, just-short-of-condescending way, as if I'm slightly slow.

"I'm waiting for some blood test results," I offer, in case she hasn't noticed I'm already 'under investigation'.

"I don't think it's anything to worry about. Come back if it gets bigger or it's worrying you."

I want to shout back at her: "It's already HUGE! And it's worrying me *right now*! That's why I'm here, FFS!"

But instead I nod compliantly as before, thank her and walk out.

*

A week later, I ring the surgery for my blood test results. The receptionist takes my name and asks me to hold on. My heart's pounding out of my chest. I hope it's not the onset of a thyroid storm. After a minute I hear a rustling noise as she settles back at the desk, followed by the buffeting of the receiver as she grabs it and puts it to her ear.

"All the tests came back normal."

"Normal", I repeat, pointlessly.

"Yes, normal. Alright?" She sounds anxious to get on with something more important.

"Yes... er...fine. Thanks."

"Bye then."

So I haven't got hyperthyroid and I haven't got anything wrong with my kidneys or liver. That just leaves the menopause and more or less *everything else* in the whole of the medical dictionary that I leafed through for a while in a bookshop yesterday. I return to the internet, like a binge-eater to the smorgasbord. I google some more variations on the theme of menopause + symptoms. It's all bad. There's an American site that describes our hormones as 'nature's armor' and lists just some of the ways that womens' bodies fall victim to disease the moment our oestrogen levels drop. 'Post-menopausal risks to female health include cancer, macular degeneration, bladder infections, osteoporosis...' I close the window.

Then there's the article about how menopausal women have to avoid sleeping *too much or too little*, or they risk stroke and heart disease. What?! The idea that even something as safe and life-preserving as sleep might have become an enemy to my cardio-vascular system is nothing short of terrifying. I start to realise what kind of risks to my health I've been storing up, ready to invade me the moment my periods grind to a halt. I'm glued to my expensive typing chair, a rabbit in Armageddon's headlights, as I contemplate the obstacle course of chronic syndromes that is now my unavoidable destiny.

The phone rings. It's Maj, who's about to walk into town from her tiny-but-perfect-realm to meet me for another go at Christmas shopping. I've already told her about what I *haven't* got wrong with me, pointing out that this means I'm back at square one on whether my symptoms are down to The Change or not. She soothingly suggests a glass of wine and a chat as soon as we've ticked off a few pressies.

As I walk down Gaol Hill, past the Salvation Army band in full regalia playing bright, brassy Christmas classics to jaded shoppers, I find myself wishing I could be more like Maj. She's got really nice hair *and* a lovely neck and eyes. She sings in a really cool choir. She smokes, but only very occasionally. She drinks, but only two or three times a week at most, and never more than two and a half glasses of wine in any 24 hour period. She walks every day for at least three quarters of an hour. She has regular acupuncture to keep her chi in balance. She's got a fabulous new extension on her house. She's even saving regularly for her pension. But much more than any of these things, right now I want to be like her because she's *two whole years younger than me.*

I've got age-envy. This is distressing and pathetic in itself. I used to like being my age. Up to now, I've tended to think that there's been *something* good about all ages and stages, more or less. But that's over. Now I'm mortal, vulnerable. I'm on the brink of losing my fertility and with it my mental equilibrium, my effectiveness, my sanity, my health and my chances of ever looking and feeling okay in slim-fitting woollen clothing again. I feel disqualified. It's all over, basically, unless either I can reverse time, or discover the secret of immortal life, or... I get pregnant again in the very near future, thereby staving off redundancy *and* the loss of oestrogen with a massive, if temporary, overdose! I suggest this putative remedy to Maj while we examine ludicrously overpriced festive candles in a designer homewares shop. She walks back around the candle display, fixes me with a look of regal authority and says:

"You must be f***ing joking, darling".

***

3. NEW DREAR (JANUARY)

Of course I don't want to be pregnant again... Do I?

It's my first day back at work after the Christmas break. I'm at my desk, staring at my laptop and a half-written story premise. The cursor is blinking at me, faux patiently. "Whenever you're ready...", it's saying with a small, faux-patient sigh. I look away from it, out of the window into my little courtyard garden. I'm watching the sparrows – a ragged band of tiny, ruffled brothers and sisters – hopping about in an icy, sleeting gale, staring back at me with their beady little black eyes... and starving. My stomach clenches. They're starving because of *me*. Because the birdfeeders I oh-so-generously hung in the big, spiky bush opposite my window are empty, except for the odd moldy nut. I haven't refilled them since *last winter*. I've lulled those vulnerable, innocent little creatures into total dependence on those nuts as their food source, and then, like a torturer dangling the promise of kindness in front of his agonised victims, I've betrayed them, abandoning the pathetic little band to their fate, and... STOP!

I swallow down my guilt-spike with the rest of my homemade cappuccino and stare at the cursor blinking on my screen again. Whenever, whenever, whenever...

Normally on my first day at work after the break I'd be beavering away with renewed vigour and purpose. True, I'd also be fighting off reality-check gloom about the price of dishwasher tablets, the arrival of Winter (laughing evilly as it warns 'the worst is yet to come'), the seasonal overspend and the fact that someone as utterly wrong as The Donald can wield so much power over all our lives. All this would normally be offset, though, by an optimistic wishlist of new year possibilities, such as a cure for all cancers, a commission to write my own TV series, an end to old-school party politics in Britain, Norwich City FC parking themselves in the Premier League forever or, more realistically, the eventual return of British Summer Time. On top of that I'd normally be reminding myself that I'm incredibly lucky: at least going back to work doesn't mean yoking myself to a life of badly-paid drudgery and exploitation.

But optimistic isn't working today. It isn't even getting in the door with the offer of a second cappuccino. Because forget short-term gloom, I've got serious, I-can't-even-be-bothered-to-brush-my-hair-because-it's-so-crap-anyway blues. I feel becalmed. And guilty. And confused. And very, very bored with worrying about my health, which, fortunately, hasn't been something I've had to focus on much up until now. I feel in need of a reset button, like the one Hilary Clinton once produced to re-boot US relations with Russia, only a lot more effective. But where and how do I find one, if pregnancy is out of the question?

I swivel away from my blinking lappie and wander back through the mental mists of time. 1982. My son, O, was conceived while his father and I were living in beautiful, rugged Nowhere, Northumberland. We'd decided to leave university a year early to demonstrate our disgust with elitist educational establishments and spend more time doing what really mattered: discussing gender equality issues, demonstrating against apartheid and nuclear power, growing our own veg and generally distancing ourselves from the Thatcherite project. M found work as a woodsman on an ancient Northumbrian estate, and I (because as a Londoner I lacked any country-type skills whatsoever) cleaned well-off people's houses.

We lived in a tiny estate hamlet, in a four-room, stone, tied cottage provided by the landowning Squire, who lived up to his benevolently wacky stereotype by walking into our cottage whenever he liked, lecturing us regularly on the enriching properties of leaf mold and, for our first Christmas there, giving us two (small) bags of his five-year-old firewood and a very large, warm, newly-scragged chicken.

Grateful though I was that we now had something to cheer up the barley and miso stew I was serving up for Christmas otherwise, I was very unused to seeing a chicken in any other condition than thoroughly dead, naked and limp, with its legs tied and stuffed into the hole where it's neck once was, wrapped up in sterilizing plastic – so I was more than a bit freaked out. Because M was at The Big House staff xmas drinks, and I'd seen other people do it once or twice, I summoned up all my back-to-the-land chutzpah and managed to decapitate, pluck and even gut the freshly-dead fowl without retching more than about ten times. Triumphant, I washed the gory result off in the sink, spent an hour chasing down draught-borne clusters of tiny chicken feathers round the cottage, and by the time M got back, I'd wrestled the bird onto its back and crammed it and its unwieldy legs into the tiny range oven in the cottage's front room.

Half an hour later, with a reassuringly familiar, chickeny smell pervading the room, I decided to baste the bird. I'd already noticed that it wasn't soft and limp like most supermarket versions, but I hadn't understood that it was 'a scratcher', a semi-feral feathered friend with attitude, who'd lived a proper outside life, developing serious beefcake while fighting off its many natural, Northumbrian predators. Neither had I taken account of the fact that, due to the large size of the chicken and the concomitant problems getting it into the oven, its legs were now braced hard against the inside of the oven door.

As I knelt in front of it and swung the door open, the sudden release of counterpressure caused our Christmas dinner to leap out past my shoulder and belly-slide over the sooty tiled floor, to lodge itself firmly under a table, amongst towers of books and the pile of smelly, raw sheep's wool I'd been trying with minimal success to turn into yarn. We cleaned the bird up, wrestled it back into the oven and we even tried eating some of it later, but the meat was so toned you'd have needed the gnashers of a Great White to do it justice.

A year later, by which time I'd fully mastered plucking and gutting without vomiting even once, we moved to an old shepherd's cottage in the middle of a field, about a quarter of a mile from Hadrian's wall, atop a huge, bare hill that looked North towards Kielder Water and south to the Northern Pennines and the Lake District. That was the upside. The downside was that the cottage had no electricity or plumbed-in toilet. Within weeks of getting pregnant, the smell of the Elsan porta-loo and the necessity to regularly dig our own excrement into the field became completely unbearable to my hyper-sensitised nose. On top of that, our family doctor in London told my Mum that I'd be mad to risk having my first child delivered in the middle of a field by my Radical Midwife friend. I stupidly believed him. We skidaddled back to London and the corrupting comforts of Southern life.

Pregnancy itself was okay, though, after the initial few weeks of spewing spontaneously, 24/7, into increasingly inappropriate vessels (a flower-bucket at a supermarket; my Mum's favourite porcelain jug; an open sack of cat litter; a stranger's welly at a party). And the middle few months were pretty cool. I felt well, I'd managed to avoid stretch marks up to that point, my hair grew much more quickly and thickly than normal (but only in normal places), everyone was nice to me because of my noticeable but not gargantuan bump and I was sporting the size of tits I'd always wanted (though they turned out to be too heavy and in the way of everything to put up with permanently).

I had food cravings, but they were for easy–to-justify, easy-to-access stuff like satsumas and watercress and porridge. I also went to a weekly pre-natal exercise class run by the National Childbirth Trust and allowed myself to be thoroughly duped into the idea that having inner peace, well-stretched inner thigh muscles and practising breathing exercises with my partner would render my labour spiritually uplifting as well as painless. LIARS. But I didn't know that until it was way too late to back out. In fact, the very first thing I said to M after giving birth, following two days of fairly unmitigated labour-ward hell, was 'please promise that if I ever forget, you'll remind me that I NEVER EVER want to do that again!'

It's different now, but this was the eighties. Right from the start of labour, I'd been the subject of some snarky wind-ups from the midwives for mentioning a natural childbirth (although in fact all I'd requested was *as* natural a childbirth as was practical, possible and safe). Not that this reasonable codicil cut any ice with sneering midwife no.1: "So *you're* the one...", was how she greeted me. Sneering Midwife One (and indeed all the midwives who followed her on the rota) then proceeded to deny me food and water or anything you could realistically call care for much of the ensuing 48 hours – those were bad old days back then.

On initial arrival in the Maternity Unit, I'd been told I was the lucky one because I was going to be the first labouring mother-to-be to use the new high-tech birthing bed they'd just taken delivery of. They'd decided to call it the King Edward VII bed for reasons I couldn't fathom, but that wasn't what was mostly worrying me as I was being walked into the labour room. Nevertheless, I was disappointed to discover that the only difference between King Edward VII and the other surgical trolley beds I'd seen was that the King was a meagre few inches wider, and had inbuilt hydraulic lifting devices so that the midwives didn't get bad backs while looking up your over-stretched vagina. In any case, having settled me onto this piece of equipment, the midwives disappeared for most of the duration (afterwards the explanation was that it was 'a bad 48 hours' on the Labour ward), leaving the petrified father-to-be to steer me through the nightmare as best he could.

Once I'd finally achieved motherhood and been wheeled back onto the maternity ward with baby O, I was so hungry and thirsty that, although I'd missed official breakfast time, I asked the only visible staff member if there was any chance of a cup of tea and a piece of toast. My request provoked a sort of fast-freeze on the face of the auxiliary nurse clearing away breakfast a few beds down from me. She stopped in mid-plate-scrape and stared at me for what seemed like hours with a mixture of disbelief and outrage. I asked again very politely and tried to look like a worthy cause for sympathy – not hard after two nights and a day spent doing the equivalent of shitting a watermelon. She carried on staring for a bit, daring me to withdraw the request. But I'm starving. Literally. I hold her look. Finally, she drops her plate-scraper and marches off.

Ten minutes later, the double doors to the ward crash open and I see the nurse coming back with the air of someone recently returned from an expedition to find Earth's last surviving meal, which I, in my utter selfishness, am intent on having all to myself. In one hand is a cup of something I'm hoping is hot and tastes roughly like tea; in the other, a plate covered with a metal keep-it-warm lid. She marches up to my bed, plonks the tea down on the bedside unit, pushes my bed-tray across in front of me and lands the plate on it with a clatter. Then, with a glare that suggests she should be getting an official decoration for this, she whips the metal lid off the plate under my nose, revealing a slick, sloppy puddle of something grey and knobbly that might once have been mince in gravy. The smell of it rises. The moment that happens, I vomit the pint of water I've just stolen from my neighbour's bedside unit and guzzled before anyone could arrest me, straight onto the plate, the tray, the bed, and the auxiliary nurse's shoes.

I wasn't allowed home from the hospital for five days, due to the terrible job they'd done sewing me up after the watermelon had finally popped out. And I swear that if that sadistic auxiliary could have kept me on nil-by-mouth as a punishment for the whole of that five days, it would have made her *year*.

I was naïve enough to think that the moment I got out of there and got home, life would fall neatly forward into the happily-ever-after category. Little did I realise the epic struggle that sleep deprivation, hormone storms, housemates *and* parenthood were about to make of my easy-peasy little existence up to then. But that's another story...

*

Despite all the above being burned into my memory forever, now that I'm facing imminent loss of options in the procreating department, I suddenly feel the urge to grab back the initiative and review my decisions. Should I, could I, would I...? I construct mental vimeos exploring what it would be like if I *really was* pregnant again: the moment where I tell O that I'm about to 'complete the family' when he's talking about starting his own is kind of embarrassing; the bit where I have to explain yet again to a woman in the supermarket that 'I'm NOT the baby's grandmother!' is depressing. Then there's the one where I exit the bathroom with a tester stick and give S the news that he's going to be a father after all, and that ends abruptly with a lot of shouting, slamming of doors and accusations of insanity.

But if pregnancy is out, what am I going to do to avoid, evade, mitigate, control or fight this middle-ageing menopausal thing? I stop in mid-mental ramble as it occurs to me that stopping it isn't even on the playlist. Alea iacta est. The future has become a known quantity. In fact, while I've been busy doing the washing up and telling the odd murder story, more than half my life's story has been pouring into the jelly-mould of existence and setting hard, beyond my ability to reshape it. I retail this grim revelation to Maj as she sits drinking Earl Grey in my sitting room, while I undress the Christmas tree. Even putting the decorations away is giving me wistful, age-related stress, along the lines of: what happened to the year that's just past? Why is Time apparently speeding up?

"Isn't age all about how you feel?" she asks, her lovely face poised at an angle on her long neck, framed by a sexy new haircut.

"Isn't that the kind of thing *young* people say?" I'm not in the mood to be easily placated.

She chuckles.

"You're still in your prime, darling. And anyway, I know loads of fabulous women in their sixties, seventies, even eighties," she insists. "Some of whom have started whole new lives for themselves."

"Name one."

Maj smiles again, unperturbed.

"What about the woman at that authors' party?"

True, I'd recently met a charismatic author in her sixties, who had gone *to Poland* to learn how to drive real passenger trains – a lifetime's ambition – and was now a part-time steam train driver for North Norfolk's Bure Valley Railway.

"And you're barely post-50 – not that you even look it," she adds quickly. "Nothing's over."

"Except my dreams," I persist gloomily.

Even Maj has to admit that I've probably run out of time to transform myself into an Olympic triathlete or a highly sought after criminal barrister… or revolutionise British education… or discover a supreme talent for body jamming. The fact is though, that up until about yesterday, I'd been harbouring fantasies about where my life *could* go that date back to about 1980. All that intervening time, I'd been blindly ignoring the ever-more-trodden path of existence that work and life had marked out for me. I'd kidded myself that I was only on that path for today, not forever. And that I had a choice about changing it.

I'm in Tesco later, feeling more than a bit grey-vote. In a queue for the tills, I spot one of the city's many 'characters', a talkative, octogenarian ex-astro-physics professor with a preference for dressing like a bag lady, eating most of her meals at Côte and wearing a selection of comical knitted hats, all with ears. As I stare blankly at the magazine stand opposite, I wonder what pushed her over the line from intense to more or less batty – could it have been the menopause? I don't dare ask her, though.

Staring back at me from the covers of the womens' mags on the nearby stand are the timelessly air-brushed-beautiful faces of older women celebs. I have a mild eureka moment. If I can't row back the missed years, the menopause or the associated onslaught of ageing, maybe I can *hide the evidence.* I've never spent much time or money on my looks before, beyond the basics. I wear basic makeup and go to the hairdresser three times a year on average. I book a mani-pedi occasionally and I like nice clothes, but I have relatively few opportunities to wear them since I spend most working days alone in my office in tracksuit bottoms and hoodies. I don't wax or self-tan or diet or buy exercise-at-home DVDs. I don't do eyebrow threading or Zumba or charity triathlons. But now what I'm thinking is that *all that stuff* and more is available if I want it, and some of it might be worth deploying in the struggle to at least feel and look like I'm shoring up the ebb tide of life.

I leaf through the mags. They're full of photos of women like Jane Fonda who are decades older than me but looking twenty years my junior. Some are botoxed, nipped and tucked up the wazoo, but there are some who claim to have kept their youthfulness simply through achievable means like drinking less coffee, watching their diet and their stress, getting regular exercise and eating royal jelly. Just like Maj in fact.

I arrive home, sweaty but energized, with bags.

"What've you been buying at Sports Direct?" S asks with genuine interest. Sports shops usually mean new footballs to him. Exciting.

"I've got some trainers and a couple of badminton rackets. I thought we could start playing again, like we used to when O was younger."

"Nice idea... but I don't really want to risk the knees until the footy season's over..." he says apologetically.

"Okay, I'll go with Maj."

But she doesn't fancy it that much either. I call O's girlfriend, F. She's an ace tennis player, though she says she's never really played badminton.

*

On court a couple of days later, I reckon I'm looking the part, pretty much. My trainers are bright and bouncy, my tracksuit looks realistic and the shuttlecock is no match for my imitation of an overhead smash.

"You're s'posed to use your wrist, not your arm," F instructs me briskly as I try my smash out.

"I thought you didn't know a thing about playing badminton." I don't *actually* say this, but it's what I'm thinking.

"Oh, right, okay."

"Shall we play a game, or just knock up?" F asks.

"May as well play a game." I'm not bad at badminton so I'm fairly confident I can hold my own against a beginner.

An hour later, I stagger in the front door and catch myself in the hall mirror. My hair is plastered crisply to my head with dried sweat. All visible skin on my body has taken on a kind of traumatized, dirty pink and grey marbling. I've got a bulging, red welt ploughing a diagonal path across my forehead and a slightly blackening eye socket, all incurred while failing to notice that I was on a direct collision course with one of the heavy-duty metal net-posts, while running for a shot. And to top off the look, the sweat stains on my tracksuit suggest someone who's just run to Norwich *from Addis Ababa*. S bounces into view down the stairs with an empty mug and a big smile.

"Cup of tea, light of my life?"

"How did you recognize me?" I'm still looking at my hideous self in the mirror.

He kisses me anyway. "How was the badminton?"

"I don't know... I was too busy trying not to slip over in lakes of my own secretions to notice."

"Good work out, though," S offers optimistically. "What's that on your face?"

I shrug. "Self-defence self harm..." I re-enact hitting myself with the rim of my racket. "I was warding off the net post."

He looks sympathetic. "Not an unmitigated success then."

"F hardly even moved her feet and she was still better than me."

"How much better?"

"We played two games to 21. I scored three points in all."

He shrugs. "You went for the exercise, not the glory."

"The one time she actually cut loose and played a shot, the shuttlecock broke the sound barrier as it passed me..."

"She's twenty five years old and an ex-tennis coach, what did you expect?"

What did I expect? Was I hoping for the spirit of Jane Fonda to enter my body and render me taut and athletic in the space of a single forty-minute session? Hell yes, actually.

"Are you going again?"

"Mmmm. Next Monday".

"Good".

"Mmmm..." But I can already see myself making some pathetic excuse and dipping out.

*

I've made myself go again, twice. And to be fair, it's been okay. I haven't died on court; F actually had to take her fleece off during the last game because she was feeling 'a bit warm', and the exercise has helped me sleep a bit better, maybe. The welt on my forehead has died right down too, so I don't look like someone's swapped my face for a National Speed Limit Applies sign any more. But the truth is, I'm really not sure that badminton's the answer. It's fun, but is it rejuvenating? Not after the warm glow of physical effort wears off and you can feel all your joints complaining, it isn't. I wonder if I should follow Maj's regime, and go for a long walk every day, or reduce my consumption of alcoholic units, but in the meantime I google 'women + rejuvenation'.

This is a revelation, but not the kind I'd hoped for. Eighty percent of the first four Google pages are offering *vaginal* rejuvenation *with a laser*, which is beyond horrific and, to my mind, must be all too easy to get wrong. There are some sites that offer facial or follicle rejuvenation, and others selling entirely implausible stuff such as wheat grass juice or Tuscan-barefoot-earth-breathing-ritual. I click on more sites, with ever more extreme, miraculous, speedy and expensive solutions. It's fatally attractive – like an unguarded tower of Pringles. My interest lasts a good hour, until, as an alternative to taking our gas and electricity readings and getting our energy bill paid, I click on a site entitled 'Liposuction Gone Wrong'. OMG.

***

4. SMOKING GUN (FEBRUARY)

I've always loved smoking – embarrassing though that is to admit these days. I started in my early teens with a deservedly now-defunct brand called Number Six (Numbies, as the cognoscenti used to call them) that we used to sneak off to 'enjoy' on The Common after school. One of my guiltiest memories of being that age is when me, Caroline and our mate SJ stopped a kindly looking lady on the street and told her a hurriedly constructed lie about how SJ's mum had been in a car accident and was being taken to the hospital but we didn't have the money for a telephone call to find out how badly hurt she was. It was a rubbish deception that didn't even make sense – if we didn't have money for a phone call, how, in the days before mobiles, did we know about SJ's mum's pretend predicament in the first place – but the woman was completely taken in and handed over the cash straight away, which we immediately exchanged for ten Numbies.

I can still remember how they tasted – like smoking dried poo laced with pepper – but we were so pleased with ourselves that we had two each, then SJ recovered the stubs to add to the horrific collection she kept hidden, in case of need, in a chest at the bottom of her bed. (SJ's dad was a thoracic surgeon who thought he could scare SJ out of smoking via compulsory visits to the operating theatre's viewing gallery to watch him perform on diseased lungs – so of course she smoked more than any of us put together.)

Once I got past feeling dizzy all the time, smoking quickly turned into one of the things that defined me. It made me edgy and grown up – so I thought – and it was an essential accessory when you were in a pub with your mates or an older boy, pretending to be 18 (or at least a lot older than you really were). When Caroline and I were in our mid-teens we graduated to Gitanes (the ones with the blue smoke and the gypsy) and people used to think we were *really* cool. *I* used to think we were really cool.

Although the cool fag-fantasy image perished years ago, I haven't had a problem with smoking a few a day up to now. It's a reward for the long hours I spend at the desk. It's a friend in need. S smokes too and is of the same opinion. But obviously there *are* consequences. So over the past few years I've occasionally thought about giving up – and even occasionally had a go at it, to see what it would be like. Horrible. Miserable. A denial of my right to kill myself how I want.

But like everything else in my whole life right now, the imminent or actual arrival of The Change is changing everything. Even my attachment to the notion that I have the right to die in a manner of my own choosing is being strangled by fear. One night late, when I'm awake on my interminable sweat, freeze, viral list, guilt and stress vigil, I confront the simple fact that, added to all the other health dangers I now appear to be facing, continuing to smoke is like deciding to swim The Channel strapped to a railway sleeper.

I wake S up. He's got to help me get a death-avoidance strategy sorted out, now. I shake him but he doesn't respond. So I kiss him awake – a nasty trick but necessary in the circumstances. He struggles up onto an elbow with a sleepy, expectant smile, but I quickly get the impression that he doesn't feel like discussing quitting smoking and who our executors should be if one or both of us dies suddenly. I don't care, though. Some things – indeed right now, almost everything – is more pressing than sleep.

"I'm just really worried about what we're doing to ourselves – voluntarily!"

"Tell me about it, I'm a Spurs fan."

"I'm serious, we're getting older – we're not immortal."

"No kidding."

"But I mean what if something happened *soon,*" I persist.

S frowns. "Tonight? This week?" Still half asleep, he's slow to pick up on the utter seriousness of this.

"Yes!"

"Oh right. I didn't realise we had a firm date with eternity. Or are you going it alone?"

"You know what I'm saying," I retort irritably, impatient to get onto the substantive issues.

"You know what, babe, I really don't. And I'm very tired, and on a morning deadline for that report. Any chance we can we do kissing and going back to sleep now, and get round to discussing dying tomorrow?"

*

Self-delusion is mankind's greatest gift to itself. By one o'clock the next day, I've entirely buried my panic about the relationship between smoking, menopause and mortality and I'm sitting opposite S in a little brasserie on the Unthank Road, enjoying the luxury of a glass of wine on a weekday lunchtime, and staring out imperviously into the grey rain, cheerily anticipating the arrival of O (whose birthday it is) and F. For the next three hours or so, I'm looking forward to indulging myself in that happy family feeling, enjoying the food, the company and the odd squeeze of my thigh from S under the table, while we celebrate O and discuss their future plans for work, life and travel.

My lightness of being is untroubled by a brief overheating episode – I've got flexible layers on – and contentment prevails through the starter, and into the main course anticipation phase, at which point S announces that he needs an inter-course fag. And so do I. We excuse ourselves – O and F are far too intelligent to smoke – and go outside to stand under the restaurant awning to light up. It's still raining and the wind's blowing my wrap away, forcing me to clutch it tightly round myself. S starts coughing. I turn away from the spluttering stream of his smoke and catch myself in a mirror hung on the narrow inside wall of the restaurant's bay frontage.

A fag hag is nasty slang for a straight woman who hangs out with gay men, I know, but it's the phrase that occurs to me suddenly as I see myself, hunched over, clutching my wrap to my ever-thickening torso, frowning into the rain with wrinkly, sunken-cheeked ill-humour as I puff away desperately on my fag. I look awful: sad, bad and somehow *incredibly* twentieth century. Shocked, I drop the cigarette and crush it under my foot. I straighten up and tell S that I'm not waiting for him.

Back at the table, still in shock, I can smell my own acrid waft as I sit down. I haven't experienced that level of mythbusting trauma about my appearance since, aged ten, I stepped into the needlework cupboard in school to see what I looked like in the kaftan thing I was embroidering. The whole interior of the cupboard was lined with mirrors so you could see yourself in 360 degree detail, which is how I discovered that when viewed side on, my nose protruded so far and so sharply from my face that I looked more like a parrot with hair than a person. I decide not to announce anything to O and F (just in case I change my mind) but I tell myself firmly, as my liver and sage tagliatelle arrives, that I've had enough of fear and ugliness and doctorly disapproval and feeling like last century's thing. I'm giving up smoking.

*

Two weeks later I'm not so much climbing the walls, as drowning in sink holes of self-pity and grumpiness so deep that not even S's offer of daily foot-massage sessions *for ever* can get me to climb out. I *hate* him for smoking when I can't. I can't sit at my desk for more than two minutes without getting up again, overcome by fidgets, irritation and desperation to inhale something stronger than the smell of my tenth coffee. I'm getting little or no work done as a result. I'm putting on weight faster than the global population is growing. I *hate* my life without cigarettes. It's not just giving me constipation, horrible dreams and a bad case of *globus hystericus* – a stress-induced lump in the throat that has had me back at the doctor's – it's actually warping my fundamental values.

I see everything now, through the prism of my deprivation. I stare at people smoking on the street with barely disguised, hostile envy. I even envy people *on television* who are smoking. My friend the Big Issue seller is an emaciated, drunken addict, horribly scarred by years of beatings and bad luck, with black stumps for teeth and hair that looks like it's been torn off and reattached in strands with blobs of glue – but now he looks to me like the luckiest man on earth, because he's got half a soggy roll-up clamped to his bottom lip... and a lighter!

I'm angry and miserable and sad beyond measure. And the stress seems to have triggered not so much a thyroid storm as a prolonged sweat event on such a fine trigger that I can't move without a break out. If I even *think* about sweating, it starts. Back on the net, I spot an article that calls hot flushes 'power surges' – a lame and unconvincing attempt to make a heat rush sound positive and empowering. Bollocks. Losing control of your internal temperature gauge is like having pneumonia. There's *absolutely nothing* good about it. And to add to my stress, I've been asked to come to a meeting in London to make a pitch for an episode of a series I don't know well, to people I've never worked with before. At least I'm not having a period...

*

Determined not to be hijacked by my physiology, I plan the logistics of my work-hunting trip with military attention to detail. I begin by booking a first-class seat on the train – unlike in second class, the carriages in first might just have cleanish, useable loos with working sinks and taps in case of emergency, and the carriages also have curtains for the windows so you don't cook (and sweat) if the sun shines through them. I stock up on nuclear strength anti-perspirant, a ten-pack of travel tissues and a medicine cabinet's worth of feminine paraphernalia. I decide on dark, slimming trousers under a cool, cotton, mid-blue shirt and short, tailored, waist-flattering black jacket. I call Caroline and arrange to spend the night with her afterwards, to avoid the commuter trains home full of farty, guffawing, half-cut men in suits.

On the day, the train travel goes well. I sit with my curtain drawn, calmly re-reading the series 'bible' and drinking coffee (with the lid on, so as not to risk pouring it down the front of my shirt on the rocky stretch of track just after Colchester). The train arrives early, so I nip into Boots to buy one more pack of travel tissues. From Liverpool Street, I catch the tube. It isn't even raining when I get out at Caledonian Road and navigate towards the address I've been given using my phone's GPS. When I get there, though, and I've walked up the street's entire length – at least a quarter of a mile – the offices don't seem to be there.

Do *not* panic, I tell myself firmly. I retrace my steps all the way back up the street. It's a messy jumble of Victorian and twentieth-century buildings and small industrial units, so there are few numbers to spot, but I'm sure I haven't missed the sign I'm supposed to be looking out for. I'm also supposed to be there by now so I'm getting hot and fretful. Turning up tardily for a first meeting with new potential 'clients' is how *not* to impress, I mutter to myself. I get out my phone, find a general number for the production company and call it, hoping for easy-to-follow instructions. No such luck. The girl manning the phones is, she tells me with aggravatingly squeaky-voiced cheerfulness, talking to me from their Gray's Inn Road HQ and she's new and there's nobody around and she hasn't got a clue how to direct me to their production offices.

Shit.

Lack of nicotine, combined with, I'm guessing, chronic oestrogen depletion, is sky-rocketing my blood pressure along with my body temperature. Sweat sprouts on my upper lip, my temples and cheekbones, and under my chin. I can feel the stuff running down my neck. My armpits are soaking. I stop to tissue down but it doesn't really help. I'm burning up and starting to panic. Which is when I notice the huge sign I'm supposed to be looking out for, attached to a building opposite.

Relieved but furious with myself for failing to see it the first time round, I hurry across the road and through the gates of what looks like an old school building. I find the entrance, rush inside, announce myself to the receptionist and am shown into a small, neon-lit, overheated, windowless office to wait. Glad of a moment to compose myself but radiating heat like a microwaved potato, I take off my coat and jacket to give myself a chance to cool down. But it's already too late. My crisp, cool mid-blue shirt is now dotted all down the front with spreading, dark, wet patches. Much worse, the whole underarm area of the shirt on both sides is stained in a burgeoning, dark circle.

I'm briefly distracted by the observation that the stain under my right armpit appears to be considerably bigger than the one under my left – does one side of my body sweat more than the other? – but the thought freezes as I get a small mirror out of my bag to check my makeup and catch the whole ensemble of sweat-soaked shirt and greasy face. I look like I'm ready for my next scene in *Ice Cold in Alex* except I'm in North London not fricking North Africa.

I wipe my face *again* and put my jacket back on, but the immediate result is that I start sweating under my eyebrows as well as everywhere else, so I take the jacket off again. Fighting off bursting into tears, I decide the best/only thing to do is position myself at the small conference table with my arms forward of, and pressed tightly to my body, elbows leaning on the table. That way, as long as the people I'm meeting sit directly opposite me, they might not see the shameful stains. I sit at the table and adopt the position. It kind of works, as long as I don't move at all.

I make another effort to compose myself. Perhaps they'll take so long to join me that I will have stopped sweating. (I've noticed that my own body heat is at least starting to dry out the smaller spots of sweat on the front of my shirt.) Perhaps they'll be incredibly understanding. Perhaps they'll be fifty-something, female and peri-menopausal. Then I remember they're called Jake and Tom. Then the door opens and Jake and Tom bundle in, laughing conspiratorially about something as the door closes behind them. My heart sinks. Not female and definitely not fifty, they barely manage the age of majority between them. And their manner is boisterous, Brazilian-barbecue-eating, new-man-macho.

"Elizabeth-Anne? Hi, I'm Jake. "

"I'm Tom. Hi".

"Hi".

Tom leans slightly over the table towards me, stretching out a hand to shake mine. Now I'm screwed. Either I ignore the hand, which will appear rude at best, or I have to reach up and out, exposing the ghastly right arm sweat stain to two very young men I've never met but on whom paying our mortgage nevertheless depends. I try to reach his hand without unclamping my upper arm from my body, but I can see Tom glancing at Jake – has she got some kind of disability? – so I unclamp, grab Tom's hand and give it a quick, damp tug. Jake extends his hand too. I repeat the movement. There's a flicker of eyes towards my armpit.

"Are you feeling okay? Do you, er, want a drink of water or anything?"

"No, I'm fine," I lie ridiculously, smiling.

Then, as both of them look at me, clearly unconvinced, I instantly wish I could rewrite the response. I should've said: "Yes that would be great, actually I just jogged from the tube." Or: "Thanks, a pregnant woman got stuck in a lift on my way here, and I had to climb forty flights to help." Or something like that. Anything like that. But along with my temperature control, my professional poise has taken a walk.

"Okay – so Elizabeth-Anne, why don't you start by telling us why you want to write for our show?"

This is a standard opener.

"Sure… well, it's a great series – one of a kind in the schedules at the moment. You've got a really sharp premise and a well-established, well-loved ensemble of characters there, and I'm…"

"Actually we're planning changes," Tom breaks in briskly, "and what we're really looking for is writers who we think can move the show on in some interesting new directions."

This throws me somewhat. I'd got the opposite impression from my brief, introductory phone call with the exec producer. "I see, so… what sort of changes are you looking to make? In which areas?"

Jake and Tom shrug in unison. "We'd rather leave the page blank for your ideas on that."

Without warning or reason, an adrenaline shell explodes in my chest, cranking my heart rate. I feel like it's my first day working for Easyjet and I've just been told I'm flying the plane, not driving the trolley.

"Right, okay…"

But it's not okay. In response to this unrehearsed challenge to my creativity, I throw open the doors of my imagination, ready to whisk out some interesting thoughts, but the lights have gone out. It's just dark. No sign of an idea anywhere, good or bad. All I can think about is whether my heart's going to pop out of my chest before sweat starts dripping off my chin onto my notebook. I realise my mouth is open and close it. I try filling the awful silence by picking up my biro and nodding and staring sagely at the notebook in front of me as if I'm weighing up interesting possibilities. I spot my biro hand shaking. So does Jake. He looks at Tom. Then at me:

"If that's a problem for you..."

*

"How did the meeting go?" asks Caroline as she gets a bottle of wine out of the fridge and I sit down gratefully at her kitchen table a couple of hours later.

"I completely blew it."

"Seriously? Why?"

"I couldn't find the place to start with, and when I finally arrived, I was so sweaty, I looked like I'd swum there…"

"It can't have been that bad…"

"No, it really was. Then they announced they were looking for writers to 'take the show in some new directions'…".

"Interesting…"

"Not as it turned out," I snap back at her. She looks at me, surprised. "Sorry. Anyway, normally that wouldn't have been a problem, but… I don't really know what happened, I just flatlined. My mind went totally blank."

"So what did you do?"

"I faked feeling sick and dizzy, and told them I was going down with flu. I hoped that might explain the sweating, the shaking and the complete inability to put coherent sentences together."

"Do you think you convinced them?"

I'm no actor. I've known this ever since I was forced onto a stage in front of my whole junior school, for a play in which my only role was to break an oil painting – in fact, a large piece of painted paper stretched inside a wooden frame – over another little kid's head. This moment was supposed to provide the comic crescendo to the last act of the play, and I was so stressed about fluffing it that I managed to completely miss the kid's head with the paper and land him a poleaxing blow with the frame instead, rendering him instantly unconscious.

Panic ensued. Ambulances were called. Schoolteachers wept, wailed and worried about litigation (it was in the US). Even worse, the boy was one of a family of ten from a deprived local estate who used to get bullied by other classmates for his misfortune, and I'd mounted a quiet protest against this injustice by making an effort to be mates with him. After knocking him unconscious in front of the whole school, though, I could never convince him that I hadn't premeditated the assault as a perfect way of sucking up to the bullies with a public display of conversion to their prejudices.

Slugging back my wine at Caroline's kitchen table, I set the scene and briefly reprise my 'coming over dizzy' performance for Caroline to judge. She's my greatest supporter and normally backs up *everything* I do or say as a matter of course. But even she doesn't sound convincing as she insists I probably got away with it.

The next morning, feeling decidedly self-disgusted, I get up late and wander downstairs to the kitchen to find her, so I can moan some more.

"Feeling any better, hon?"

"Not a lot. I spent most of the night sweating, dreaming about cigarettes, and reliving the embarrassing failure of yesterday."

"Are you really that sure you screwed it up?"

"Surer than ever."

"And you think it's got something to do with this peri-menopause thing?"

"No one's yet offered a better explanation for my recent reincarnation as a brainless idiot... "

I whine on, while she makes coffee.

"I can't believe Mutsi never warned us about it all." (Mutsi was what we called our mum.)

"Well, she was on HRT right from the start," Caroline points out, "so she probably didn't know much about it."

That's a point. I hadn't remembered she took HRT. In fact, I haven't even thought about HRT…

My niece, Anna appears. She bounces over to give me a hug. As ever, I'm amazed by her: 5' 10", cover-girl looks, kind, funny, talented and clever – plus she's got the sparkliest, most all-encompassing smile of anyone on the planet. Just being the recipient of that smile gives me a lift.

"Hey, ma Tante," she says as she hugs me (she's got a place to do French at uni). "How're you doing?"

"I'm old and it's over, beautiful girl," I tell her with a hastily added smile.

"Don't be ridiculous, you're the coolest Aunty I know," she insists, with her usual generosity.

I manage another smile as Caroline passes me coffee and we settle at the table. Then the kitchen door opens again and Anna's ex-boyf, Paulo walks in and sits down with us. Paulo is strange. He's supremely polite but undisguisedly self-interested, angelically good-looking but narcissistic and effete. He spends a lot of time doing Anna's hair and helping her shop for clothes. Caroline has already explained that Anna thinks he's bi but won't admit it to himself, and that despite her having broken up with him ages ago, she has him over to stay regularly, because he's a bit of a Billy-no-mates and has a hard time at home with religiously orthodox parents.

"Me and Anna have been discussing ageing," Paulo announces suddenly, with a disingenuous smile at us old crones.

"Why…?" I snap back. Caroline shoots me a don't-let-him-wind-you-up look.

"I've already got really baggy eyes – look!"

Paulo presents his large, totally un-baggy, almond-shaped peepers to me. “Maybe I should go and see someone.”

“Yeah, I’d hurry up about it, or you’ll lose your peripheral vision along with your pulling power,” Caroline informs him, deadpan.

“No way?! That’s sick!”

He sits on his hands and stares at me for a sec.

“Have you ever thought about getting work done?”

“Work?”

“Y’know, like, cosmetic surgery.”

“No!” I protest a bit too much. “I’m barely past 50,” I add huffily.

He shrugs. “My mum has had three ops so far – plus she gets regular botox and dermal fillers – and she’s only 45.”

“Her prerogative,” I manage magnanimously.

But Paulo’s not in the mood to let me off.

“Why wouldn’t you, though? If everything’s going saggy and wrinkly…”

I ponder my response. My inclination is to punch him squarely in his not-saggy face, but Anna’s giving me a look that says 'don’t punch him squarely in his not-saggy face, he’s just an insensitive saddo'. And she’s right. I decide to give him a straight answer. As I’m saying it, I realise it’s also true.

“Actually, I can’t think of anything worse than having cosmetic surgery.”

“No way! Why?” Paulo is clearly fascinated now.

“Because ageing is hard enough to deal with on its own, anyway. The idea of waking up every morning to check out whether your bum hike is going south or your tits are slipping sideways yet is a total nightmare. I’d be four times as neurotic if I had *that* to contend with, along with all the other stuff.”

Anna grins and gives me a thumbs up.

“What other stuff?” Paulo persists, apparently still genuinely interested, but Anna cuts him off.

"Let's go get some breakfast at Pret, P – and stop annoying my nearest and dearest."

I mouth a grateful 'thank you' to Anna as the two of them get up to go. From the door, she grins back over her shoulder at me. Beautiful. I feel an injection of happiness. She's part of me, and I'm part of her, so I get to sit back, relax and share in all the exciting promise of her life, *and* bask in the reflected glory of her loveliness. Just for a minute or so – until self-disgust creeps back under the door – it occurs to me that being 50-something does have some upsides after all.

***

5. ME, MYSELF, I (MARCH)

The clocks are about to go forward and I've had an epiphany. I think. I'm still alive (but that's not the epiphany), so the odds are that I haven't got an aggressive condition or terminal disease that's going to take me off any time soon, at least not in the immediately foreseeable future. After all, over my lifetime I can bear personal witness to the existence of thousands of women over 50 who smoke or have other lethal habits, but who are, against all odds, one hundred percent alive. On the other hand, despite not managing to achieve an official diagnosis, I *am* now convinced that I'm peri or maybe even totes menopausal. And it's high time to stop fighting reality and get a serious, considered management plan sorted instead.

I formally acknowledge my situation one Sunday afternoon (while S is receiving urgently needed post-Sunday-football treatment at the Rose Tavern) with a private ceremony involving a bath filled with foam, my favourite podcast and a miniature bottle of champagne. I lie back in the water, glass in hand, toast my womanhood, and remind myself of all the amazing blessings of life: family and friends, learning and loving, the Elveden bypass, Aretha Franklin, Mr Pickering's award-winning Sicilian Mountain sausages (available at his stall on Norwich market and online) and the all-over-sunny feeling I still get when S tells me how he feels about me.

On his return from pub therapy, I tell S about my decision to get real, and he's incredibly sympathetic, a bit relieved (I can tell) and lies convincingly about how young and fantastic I look. I share with him my new rationale: life could be a whole helluva lot worse. I don't much like it, but I'm getting resigned to my new sleep(less) patterns. The hot flush and sweating problem is unpredictable from one day to the next, but at least it's no longer ambushing me. I'm mostly ready for it. The irrational anxiety and stuff, I've just got to learn to handle or at least tough out. My last bout of biological bloodletting wasn't quite as bad as the previous one, so maybe that's progress. And staying off the fags is getting a tiny bit easier, partly due to me catching a bad cold from some disgustingly sniffly kid on the Central Line on my way home from Caroline's. A couple of days in bed with a temperature and *Cash in the Attic* for entertainment provides a useful distraction from the endless convo with myself about why I can't just have one cigarette, because after all I... (any number of pathetic excuses supplied thereafter).

Now that I've accepted the basics of my 'condition', I'm less interested in wiki-diagnosing myself. I've discovered that I don't really want to know that I have vasomotor instability, skin thinning or atrophy of my genitourinary tissue to look forward to. The only exception to this voluntary info blackout is my clandestine investigation into HRT. I've realized that part of the reason no one ever warned me about the menopause is that most of my mum's generation, like her, took HRT and therefore *never experienced it*. At the time it must have looked like a no brainer: suffer the menopause and let all the dreadful consequences of oestrogen depletion into your life, or take this great little pill and stay eternally youthful. No contest. But that was then.

My investigation has to be covert because back in the 80s my generation of women were busy storming all sorts of male bastions, from pub to Parliament, and this involved, among other things, refusing to accept that everything doctors *said* was good for them really *was* good for them – hence the feminist rejection of HRT. I'm therefore not admitting it to Caroline or Maj or Lou (especially not Lou because she's a semi-qualified homeopathic practitioner and she'd give me a *really* hard time) but... I'm just taking one more, sneaky look at the pros and cons of hormone therapy.

I've discovered there are two kinds: HRT and BHRT – *bioidentical* HRT. Apparently it's an alternative 'natural' version, although the Wikipedia description is at pains to note that there's no evidence it's any safer than its non-bio counterpart. Either way, the benefits are clear and obvious. In return for a few possible side effects, most of which most women have been dealing with admirably since the time of hunter-gathering (fluid retention, bloating, breast tenderness or swelling, headaches, indigestion and depression) you get no menopausal symptoms, or, at least for most, heavily reduced ones. And therefore you get slower and fewer 'impacts' from the loss of oestrogen, which includes everything from keeping your bone density, mental acuity and regular periods, to avoiding the tendency of *pretty much everything* to get thinner, flabbier and wrinklier.

The other day I put on a pair of well-loved old jeans and was at first pleasantly surprised when I noticed that instead of being too tight round the waist now that I don't smoke, they were actually slightly slipping off my hips. Had I started losing some of my non-smoker's weight gain already? I revelled in this cheerful illusion for most of the day, until I realized, after taking a long look in the mirror and doing a few experiments, that my jeans were actually falling off my *bum*, not my hips. Critical loss of arse pertness is not included in the list of things that HRT can help you avoid, but I think it should be.

But then there are the negatives: increased risk of endometrial (uterus lining), ovarian and breast cancer; increased risk of heart disease and stroke. In other words, Hypochondria City. I don't want to go there again. So I'm going to avoid medicalisation of my problem and betrayal of my generation and try and ride the symptoms out a bit longer *au naturel*... I can always take stock in a couple of months and cave in at that stage.

Needless to say, I haven't had a call back from Jake, Tom or anyone else from Gray's Inn Road. The lads are probably still making jokes about the crazee old laydee while sucking on their craft beers and eating huge lumps of barely-cooked meat in some grillhouse round the corner from the office. But I'm over it. Mostly. And anyway, it's not a problem because I've been asked by a producer at the BBC to work up a treatment for a possible new series about 'gunbunnies' (Army slang for women in the Royal Artillery). I get paid for the work, and although the odds are thousands to one against it ever getting made as a series, I also get to do some interesting research with (hopefully) interesting women. And as a special bonus, Colchester, where a bunch of these gunbunnies is garrisoned, is only an hour away from Norwich on the train, so I'm not even required to travel too far. Result. Plus I'm hoping this will help mitigate the impact of the latest unpleasant development being imposed on my life by The Change.

There's the old me – the adult female I've been living as for the last 35 years, who is, for the most part, fairly easy going, calm and collected, efficient and decisive. Then there's the new Menopause Me, the cringingly crap one I *really can't stand*, who made her debut at the disastrous meeting in North London and can't apparently now be shaken off.

Menopause Me is very easily put off her stride. She's tongue-tied, tetchy and forgetful and has a tendency to say inappropriate things. She dithers and ditsies about. She loses things, bumps into things, can't remember whether she turned things off, and worries a lot about all of the above. I've spotted people watching her strangely, or treating her with kind condescension. Even worse is the fact that the old me is fast becoming invisible to others, *most of the time*. Menopause Me is the one everyone seems to be noticing. To be honest, I want this ditsy cow to eff off and die, preferably today. But she won't. She's getting stronger, more stupid and more tenacious every day.

Yesterday in the supermarket, I was heading away from the cashier with my trolley when I dropped my purse on the floor, bent over to pick it up, stumbled and stamped down incredibly hard on the foot of a very small, very elderly lady, then whirled round to apologise and whacked the lady's equally ancient husband in the head with my bag as he bent down to tend to his wife. A maladroit moo in a china shop.

Then, in my disarray, I forget to either apologise properly or recuperate my *whole set of keys*, attached to the little gismo you stick in the euro/pound slot of the trolley. I walk home, sweaty and sticking to myself from carrying the bags, then realize the keys aren't any longer in my bag or in any of my pockets or, for the second and third time of looking, in my bag or in any of my pockets! S is out, so I have to leave tonight's fish multiplying lethal bacteria on the doorstep and go rushing back to the shop.

As I hurtle back in through the doors of the shop I spot myself in a large mirror: I'm dripping in sweat, and I've got the manic, hunted look of Basil Fawlty trying to cover up his latest lie. The nice man who spotted my keys stuck in the trolley while I was gone turns out to be the long-suffering husband of the woman whose big toe I'd crushed. He'd noticed the keys while waiting for the taxi they'd ordered to take them home, because his wife can't walk on the toe. They wouldn't even let me pay for the cab, so keen were they to get away from the madwoman. Humiliation complete.

*

Today – I'm hoping – MMe will be leaving well alone. S and I are trustees of a small charity that works with young people in danger of social and/or educational exclusion and we've got a meeting with a local businessman who we're hoping to persuade to donate some much-needed cash. We're walking down to the local indy cinema where we're rendezvousing with Mr. Business for coffee. I'm moaning.

"I'm freezing, can you put your arm round me."

S complies enthusiastically.

Half a minute later: "Actually ..." I pull away suddenly. "I'm getting hot now."

I pull at my scarf as heat pricks my neck.

"I'm not feeling too good. Light headed. Like I might faint."

"Want me to do the meeting on my own?" S offers.

"I don't want to go home alone if I'm going to faint en route," I retort spikily.

"Okay, we'll keep it short. I'll do the talking if you like."

"Wish we'd got a cab there now. I'm sweating buckets", I huff. I pull off my scarf and undo the top button of my jacket.

He slows his pace. "Want to go slower?"

"No, let's just get there," I snap back. "Then hopefully I'll have five minutes to cool down before he arrives." My tone is accusatory.

"Cheer up, chicken," S requests lightheartedly, before my icy return look shuts him up. I hate him for making light of my darkness.

Mr. Business is already there as we enter the bar, so there's no time for me to swab myself down, or calm my agitated mood, which means I'm uncomfortable and off my stride during the introductions. S suggests he should get some coffees while Mr. Business and I settle at a table. Somehow the thought of being left alone to kick off the meeting sets off a vigorous eddy of panic through me. I pull a hacked-off face at S as he walks away, then realise from Mr. Business's expression as I turn back that he's spotted it. I grin, embarrassed, open my mouth, hoping something light and disarming will pop out... but I've flatlined again. Absolutely nothing comes to mind. Mr. Business breaks the deadlock.

"Shall we sit down?"

I manage a smile. "Good idea."

My heart is pounding and I'm feeling distinctly dizzy as we sit down at a table opposite each other. I glance at S, still waiting to be served at the bar, and suppress another wave of panic. Why do I feel like I'm about to begin some kind of life or death examination of my right to exist? I tell myself to calm down and focus sufficiently to re-engage Mr. Business with another, hopefully more accomplished, smile. I start to explain what we do as a charity and why we think the kids we work with deserve help from the community, and from him. He starts to relax. So do I. He's looking at a short promo film we've made on my iPad and nodding approvingly.

"Looks like good stuff."

"Yeah, we've had really pleasing results from our in-school projects this year, all community-funded, by the way. Our ultimate goal is to expand the programme out of Norwich and run it throughout the county's schools." This is an idea we've only just thought up, but I think the ambition suits this guy's interest.

"Well that sounds like something we could potentially get behind. How much have you raised so far and what roughly does it cost per school delivery?

"Costs are variable, depending on the school and the number of students participating but ballpark a thousand pounds a day. In terms of funds already in, we've had a couple of large donations so far." More half-truths. 'Large' is a relative term.

"Of…?"

He wants to know how much. I need to provide a vague but satisfactory answer, and I've got one. But I've flatlined again. I can't find the phrase I want. I clear my throat. It just won't come to mind. "I can't… er..."

S and I have agreed in advance that if he asks this question, we'll stay vague and cite donor confidentiality, because we don't want to discourage him from giving us a decent donation. But I've lost the phrase.

"You can't…. what..?" he asks, looking puzzled.

"The issue is…I, er…" Nope. It's all spelled out there on my mental hard disc, but it's just not downloading.

"It's..." I dig desperately for a work-around word.

"Er ... secret," I stutter finally.

"A secret?"

Mr. Business's expression is quickly resolving from perplexed into openly wary. S arrives with the coffees. He glances at both of us. He can see something's up.

"Here's the coffee. So how are we doing?" he asks with a slightly over-jaunty tone.

My brain powers up unexpectedly.

"Confidential!" I blurt out.

S stares at me, for once lost for a response.

"I meant to say it's a question of donor confidentiality," I elaborate to Mr. Business, who clearly thinks I'm either lying or a total fruit-loop or both. "Some people and organisations prefer us to be discreet about the frequency and value of their contributions."

"I see," he says. But I know I've blown it.

Mr. Business barely goes through the motions for the next five minutes, before finally calling a halt to the meeting on the pretext that he's got another one to get to. We hand over our card, smile bravely and watch him go.

"Not our best performance, light of my life."

"You mean mine wasn't," I retort tetchily. "He asked the question about funds, I was trying to explain why we couldn't give details and my mind just went completely blank... it's happening all the time... driving me round the bend."

S puts a hand on my thigh and squeezes reassuringly, but I can see from his expression and slightly hangdog body language that he's finding Menopause Me pretty hard work. Join the queue, I think bitterly.

"If you're feeling that bad... I dunno... maybe you should go back to the Doc... think again about getting some treatment?"

Somehow, him even suggesting this kicks me over the line into furious. He's still squeezing my thigh. I swipe off his hand.

"Coming from someone who childishly refuses to go to the doctor *however ill he is* because, as he dumbly insists, they *might find something wrong with him*, I think you should take your suggestion and stuff it up the first available orifice!"

I stand up, grab my bag, and as S watches me with unhappy resignation, I stalk out of the bar and plod furiously home alone. S arrives a minute later. We retire to our offices, or steer as necessary round the house for the next few hours, avoiding any contact long enough to trigger further argumentative exchanges. Now I *really* feel lonely. Poor me. Is it *my* fault that I've turned into a grumpy, sweaty, brain-damaged madwoman overnight?

***

6. ALIEN INVASION (APRIL)

Is feeling insane the same as being insane? I'm hoping not. Surely, as long as I can ask myself that question, it means I'm still capable of objective thought and analysis, and that means I'm not mad. Or does it? Maybe asking myself the question is a subconscious preparation for the reality of madness. This is a thought-loop that I'm aware could easily send me insane, even if I'm not quite there yet. Luckily, as Mad March gives way to April Fools, Maj is with me to inject sense and head up an independent enquiry into this very issue.

"Of course you're not going mad, darling."

"You'd tell me honestly, though, wouldn't you?"

"I'd do more than that. No one wants a Minister of Finance who doesn't always wear matching shoes."

"Now you're taking the piss…"

"Okay, I'll be serious. Time for the all-revealing sanity questionnaire."

"Stress." And I mean it.

Maj smiles reassuringly. "Do you know what day of the week it is?"

"Tuesday."

"It's Wednesday, but that's close enough," Maj allows generously. "Next: What would you do if someone offered you a juicy commission this very day?"

"Panic and celebrate in equal measure."

"Correct within normal limits." She smiles back at my scowl. "Okay, final question: were the 9/11 attacks the work of A, aliens in league with George Bush employing their latest extra-terrestrial laser technology? B, Al Quaeda, C, the CIA, or D, the Illuminati?"

I make a face. "I'm not that mad".

"Good," says Maj. "What's your answer?"

"What was A again?"

"Funny…"

We're in Maj's car, en route to an 'activity' that Maj is convinced will divert me from my current obsession with insanity. It's a taster session for an upholstery course being run by an acquaintance of hers. Gail is a stay-at-home creative type with a rich hubby who used to 'dabble' in antiques (so she's told us, with obviously false self-deprecation). The taster is a day-long session in which we will learn the basics of how to re-cover old chairs. It's all part of the upcycling 'thrift revolution' and – seeing as how I'm a Premier League spender and Clairitanian Minister of Finance – only some of me approves of this idea. But Maj is strongly of the opinion that doing something with my hands rather than my head could have a significant impact on my unwell-being. And as always, I trust her.

We turn up at the house – a big detached palace of Victorian brickwork on Norwich's Millionaire's Row. We discover that we are two of about twenty eager upholstery virgins, all of whom Gail can't wait to patronise, under the guise of welcoming us to 'er 'umble 'ome.

"Annoying cow," I whisper to Maj snidely as Gails scatters us with cheap largesse. I contemplate slipping away before it's too late, but Maj won't let me. Okay, I tell myself. Grow up, settle down and try and get something out of this.

We're all introduced to each other and the set up for the day in Gail's enormous, Aga-driven kitchen over a cup of bitter, lukewarm filter coffee that makes my heart pound. Then we're shown through to an equally huge 'day room', with several large worktables and a selection of old chairs inviting reincarnation. First of all, Gail pairs us off. We'll need to work two to a chair, she explains firmly. I'm a bit thrown to find myself partnered not with Maj but with an eccentric-looking, white-haired, retired woman who calls herself Cat and licks her lips like one at me non-stop. Next, we're told to get out the only thing we've been asked to bring with us – a pair of scissors. Except, as I scrabble around in my on-trend, Indian recycled fertilizer-bag bag, I can't find mine.

Irritation, embarrassment and self-loathing well in me like a pop-up volcanic eruption. I can't *stand* the fact that *I'm* going to be the ditsy one who has to confess she's forgotten the *only* thing we had to remember. Cat offers to share hers, which makes me feel worse for some reason, so I start over-apologizing, telling her how utterly useless I am, how I remember taking it out of the sewing box and putting it on the hall table... how even a lobotomized kitten should have sufficient mental powers to remember... she frowns quizzically at me. I notice Maj raising her eyebrows. I realise I've said 'lobotomised kitten' – I can't explain the odd choice of analogy although I can see from Cat's expression that an explanation might be helpful. I wish I had one. Maybe it was her feline face staring at me...

But this is happening more and more often: as well as being lost for words, or rational thought, I'm also experiencing moments when my brain/mouth interface runs totally out of control...

"It's only a pair of scissors, dear," says Cat finally, trying to stem my verbal deluge. "Let's listen to what Gail has to say shall we?" The tone is firm, adult-to-child.

Half an hour later, I'm working away with Cat on a rickety, balloon-backed dining room chair. I'm having a lot of trouble seeing things close up, which isn't ideal, but I've recently realized why it is that older people look at things by holding them away from themselves and squinting: it actually *works*, even if it makes your head ache.

The upholstery of our chair's seat has been cheaply fixed to the seat frame in the past with a lot of staples, so we're pulling them out with a small staple-getter-outer-tool supplied by Gail. But this isn't all that easy and, added to the fuzzy vision, it's making me impatient. Finally, I grab the scissors and push the closed blades under one of the last remaining staples, but the blade slips and gouges a nasty hole in the forefinger of my other hand before I can pull it away. As blood and heat and mortification well up and over, I drop the scissors and grab for my bag.

"You're dripping blood on our nice fabric, dear," says Cat in a tone of mildest remonstrance.

"Shit! Sorry, I'm really so sorry, I've got tissues and a box of plasters somewhere..."

"I'm sure Gail has plasters – why don't you let me..."

I'm rummaging frantically in my bag with the uncut hand, finger-searching for the plasters...

"No really, it's okay! I've got everything here, really, it's just... ow!"

My cry, as something sharp plunges between my thumb nail and the nail bed, is loud enough to attract all the upholstery virgins' attention. My other hand, as I pull it out of my bag, is bleeding now. Watched by my fascinated audience, I drop the bag on the floor, grab it by the bottom and tip it upside down, releasing a meteor shower of miscellaneous but embarrassing items including two handheld battery-operated fans, a large, ready-rolled joint (a gift from the young guy that gardens for me, who said it did wonders for his mum), lots of escaped tampax and pads, tissue packets, more tissue packets... and finally, not just one but two pairs of scissors, one large, one small. I stare down at them, as does Cat. I look at my bleeding hands, as does Cat. I feel like a freak.

"I... I really didn't know they were there!"

"No, of course not, dear, it's not..."

"You must think I'm mad..."

"Not at all."

"Honestly, though, I *am* going mad, you wouldn't believe what it's like…"

"It's probably nerves…"

"It's the menopause, it's as if I've got…"

"You're not yourself…

She's trying to calm me down, stop me talking, but I've got to explain:

"…some kind of aliens who've taken control of me and are busy running live tests on every aspect of my being in the hope of triggering a complete mental and physical breakdown!"

I gather from their expressions as they stare at me, that the upholstery virgins are unclear whether I *actually believe* what I've just told them or not.

"Darling." Maj is at my side with tissues for my bleeding fingers.

"I've lost it, Maj," I whisper pointlessly, as the virgins turn back, murmuring, to their projects.

"I'm not disagreeing with you."

"Get me out of here?"

An hour later, I'm safe in the sanctuary of Clairitania, lying on Maj's sofa with a plaster on each forefinger, staring at her tiny-but-perfect woodburner, watching her low carbon, eco-log flames dance behind the glass. She appears with tea.

"You're a lifesaver, Maj."

"Don't exaggerate. The aliens were off to devastate Ipswich, I barely had a fight to get you back."

I manage a pathetically small smile. "What am I gonna do, though? I know I keep going on about it, but I wasn't really joking about alien abduction. I feel like a stranger *to myself*. The term 'beside myself' keeps coming to mind…"

"You need something really powerful for mind, body and spirit."

"Tom reckons that spliff might work wonders."

"Something legal might be more advisable."

"A cigarette, then."

"Something legal *and* health-giving. To centre you," she counters gently. "Yoga?"

"Doesn't work for me – all those positions you're made to get into." I add childishly: "And they've got really dumb names like '*The happy fish with a plate in its mouth*'..."

"I didn't know you'd ever been to a yoga class," Maj counters mildly.

I shrug a sulky 'whatever' in her direction.

Maj looks at me evenly. Her gaze is like a good doctor's: forensic but forgiving... and infinitely patient.

"Okay, not Yoga. What *do* you like doing that *really* chills you out?"

"I already told you. Smoking!"

"Cast your net a little wider," she insists gently.

I shrug again. "Walking, I guess... but only when it's warm, not when it's too hot or too cold... swimming, but only on holiday, outdoors... cooking, but it's the time of the year when everything comes from Peru and tastes like stale string... reading, but I can't really concentrate on anything at the moment and anyway I can't *see* a bloody thing unless I'm holding it a yard away..."

"You're screwed then," Maj says lightly.

"Yeah".

Pause.

"I guess if I can't take it any more, there's always HRT..." I float this as if it's never occurred to me before and I haven't spent hours googling it. I wait for Maj's reaction. She puts her head to one side in a noncommittal kind of way, then slides a womens' magazine, open somewhere in the middle, towards me.

"Mmmm. You might want to read that first."

I look down at the double page spread. The body of the article is in small type and therefore way too fuzzy to read, but the headline exclaims: *'Hormone therapy made me poison my Pomeranian.'*

Another shrug. "I don't like dogs anyway, especially not toy ones with sharp little feet."

"I'm not sure that was the point of the article," Maj counters. "But in the end, hon, it's a balance of risks to benefits. It's your choice to make."

And since, these days, I can't even decide what colour towel to choose without calling a three-day mental conference on the subject, I know what that means.

*

In a bid to follow through on my promise to myself to accept the realities of my age and stage, and on the urging of Maj and my sister, I'm going to stop pretending I can see anything small and close up, even in good light, and go to the optician. The encouragement from Caroline and Maj is partly selfish: they're fed up with me sending them indecipherable texts (because I can't see what I'm typing), then misreading their replies and having to sort out the misunderstandings at length over the phone later. And I think they're getting bored with reading menus out loud to me in cafés. It's depressing to admit that I *really* can't see anything clearly any more, unless it's twenty yards away. It drives me straight back to the mental waiting room signposted 'Failing Powers' – but there's an upside: attending the eye test is a solid gold displacement activity, helping me avoid thinking about our developing financial storm front.

As a freelance, I'm used to having cash flow ups and downs, about which my bank has always been extremely understanding, and for years the work's been regular anyway, so no problems. But from the one occasion recently that I dared to take a sneak peek at our account statements online, I've calculated that we've only got a few months grace before the cash flow crisis becomes the total-desertification-of-account crisis, swiftly followed, quite possibly, by the liquidate-everything-in-desperate-attempt-to-stave-off insolvency crisis.

On top of the looming financial storm there's the worry about *why* the work phone isn't ringing with its usual regularity. Just as with extreme weather events, it's hard to be sure whether this is the result of a short-term cyclical dip or a more worrying longer-term trend. And whichever explanation is right, there's an important related question I've been avoiding asking myself: have I really been *trying* to get work recently? Have I been hungry for it? Or have I been going through the motions, because I'm feeling a bit too crazy and distracted to cope with, well... anything, half the time. This thought spawns more unsettling questions. If it's my fault that the phone isn't ringing, will the lack of work become a lack of career, a withering on the crime-drama vine, the end of everything? Will it signal a final, death-knell end to over-shopping?

I'm fighting a losing battle to shut out this gloomy audit while waiting for the optician to come and call me in for my eyesight check. But in a development that is fast becoming typical of me, I realise (after about half an hour of irritable waiting) that I've managed to either misread or wrongly remember the time of the appointment, so I'm actually an hour early. So now I'm feeling stressed about wasting my own time so efficiently *and* I'm already in a well-developed state of alarm about the examination itself. Only a year ago, I would have been bored and impatient, keen to get my eyes sorted and get back to whatever deadline I was on. Now, all that everyday insouciance has gone. Instead, I'm twitchily tense, and preemptively arming myself for bad news: scouring my mental database for info about incipient blindness, brain tumours, heart disease and anything else that can be diagnosed from staring into someone's eyes.

Eventually, Rishi Sunak, or someone who looks amazingly like him, appears neatly suited, smiling and carrying a clipboard and calls my name. My toe jams the leg of a small table next to me as I get up and I stagger slightly, knocking a pile of leaflets off the table onto the floor, triggering an instant liquid break-out with a side of mental self-flagellation. The optician generously pretends not to notice my disarray as I hastily gather up and dump the leaflets back on the table and he gestures me into his cubicle.

After a few minutes of reading out numbers and letters, and staring into a kind of oversized Viewmaster, the optician tells me that, yes, both my eyes are mildly (albeit differently) longsighted so I'll need a prescription for working, reading and any close work, but that my far sight is 20/20. I'm so geared up for something more catastrophic in the way of health revelations that I stare at him stupidly for a moment and then:

"So you didn't find evidence of anything else?"

"Such as?"

The question irritates me. *He's* the optician. I'm not supposed to speculate on my own health, ocular or otherwise.

"I really wouldn't know, I just meant..."

"There was nothing in my examination to cause any concern."

"But there *was something*?"

The young man looks mildly quizzical. "I just said..."

"You *said*," I cut in firmly, spelling it out for him, "nothing to cause concern, which implies that there *was* something, but not something that would normally give rise to..."

He interrupts me with a sharp raise of eyebrows. "Ms Wheal."

I stop and look at him. The optician looks levelly back at me for a second. He opens his mouth then closes it again.

"You're perfectly healthy." The tone is patronizing. He's obviously decided I'm the 'worried well' type, but what does he know?

"Your glasses will be ready tomorrow."

"Okay, fine. Thanks".

I head back downstairs to the sales floor, relieved but annoyed at being patronized by a big-eyed, skinny child in a suit. I stop to try on the frames I've chosen once more before I leave the shop. Since booking the appointment, I'd been nursing a mild fantasy about looking cool, and maybe even looking cool *and* younger, in my new specs. O and Caroline look pretty cool in glasses. Anna wears them if she doesn't feel like putting in her contacts, and she looks AMAZING in hers. But I lucked out completely on that gene. My nose is way too big, too crooked and too narrow. My eyes are too close together. And my head is pea-sized – so small that my choice of frames has been limited to what's available in the childrens' section – and even some of those seem to swamp my whole face.

As I stare through the empty frames at the slightly fuzzy image – of a bad selfie of a camel in specs – I tell myself I've just got to accept that I'm old and ugly, and resign myself bravely to tearing down lots more dearly-held illusions and fantasies about myself in the days and months to come.

"Those really suit you, Madam. You look great in them."

It's one of the easy-smiling, pretty sales assistants, who's clearly got nothing better to do for the moment than lie outrageously to customers. "Thanks," I say. "That's cheered me up."

And I mean it. I'll swallow any titbit of hollow self-deception over the full-English of unpalatable truth any day.

*

If getting the glasses proved relatively painless, managing them has turned out to be a whole different matter. Once you've let glasses into your life, I've realized, utter dependence is quick to establish itself. It's now clear that as soon as they drop into your bag, the glasses transmit a message to your brain telling your eyes that they don't have to bother seeing *anything* unaided anymore, so you're literally blind without them. This also means there's yet another item that Menopause Me needs to remember to bring whenever I leave the building, but invariably doesn't.

Nor did I realise that you can't move position while wearing them without inducing serious levels of nausea. If you get up with them on, or even look at anything farther away than your hand, it's like Day Two on deck during Perfect Storm. But the worst thing about having glasses is the *label* that goes with it. Catching a reflection of my bespectacled self in a café yesterday, I thought I was looking at the 'old lady' next to me for a few seconds before I realised that the old lady *was me*. Just having to put a pair of glasses on to read something in a public place invites the assumption that you're a pensioner, or close to it.

I point this out moodily to S over dinner. He reacts with his customary energy and an idea for instant redress of the situation.

"If you're feeling labeled, we need to do something to fight back. Something to make you feel as young as you look again."

I harrumph, unconvinced. "Such as?"

"A game of pitch and putt at Baby Augusta?" Pitch and putt is S's solution to pretty much every sort of malaise in life's great catalogue. Baby Augusta is a shabby municipal course on Mousehold Heath, ten minutes drive away.

"It's not speaking to me."

"Okay... What about a credit-card-fuelled night of rejuvenating romance, sex and adventure out at the coast, then?"

This is much more like it. Sex and adventure may be pushing it, given my *condition*, but romance and a night of childishly ignoring my lack of remunerative work at the coast sounds great. S makes a couple of calls the next morning, we pack an overnight bag, switch off the mobiles, and drive an hour northwest out of Norwich to a gastropub hotel just behind one of Norfolk's finest beaches. The weather is cool and windy but clear, and the shimmering, pale pink and blue light in the sky as we get to the coast almost makes me cry, it's so stunning. The credit card works, the room is perfect, the lunch is great, and sitting on the beach as the tide comes in around the dunes, sharing my gardener's gift to me, makes us both giggly and in the mood for lerve.

By the time we're sitting eating breakfast the next morning, I'm looking at life through a distinctly more positive lens.

"I wish we could do this every couple of weeks."

"We can. Once a month or so anyway. We'll just have to economise on other things."

I reach out and grab S's hand over my locally smoked kippers.

"Thanks for saving me from myself, lovely man."

"If you could see you the way I see you..."

"Yeah... I caught you squinting at your screen the other day like Mr Magoo. I reckon you need Specsavers too."

We grin through the rest of breakfast, pay the bill, take a brisk walk on the beach hand in hand, and jump back in the car. I'm feeling, if not entirely rejuvenated, at least more myself and less Menopause Me than I've felt in weeks. Unfortunately, as we arrive home a couple of hours later, I realise that Menopause Me is lurking constantly, ambushing any attempts I make at escape from her.

As we walk up the path to the front door, one of our neighbours is standing at the top of our steps, looking chilly and extremely annoyed. She'd left her only set of keys with me while she went on holiday, so that her carpenter could access a door in need of rehanging, and I'd promised to be at home on the evening of her return, to give her the keys back. And that was yesterday. But as with so many details of my life right now, I'd managed to forget the promise entirely. As a result, my neighbour has been unable to get into her house and has had to spend an uncomfortable night on a friend's sofa down the road, sending me increasingly desperate and finally rude voicemails (none of which I've picked up).

And that kind of takes the edge off…

***

7. UNDER WATER (MAY)

It's officially summertime. This is a good thing – at least to the extent that I can delete car crashes in the fog, S dying from a heart attack on a footy pitch somewhere in Norfolk, and any number of other winter-related worries from my almost infinite list of going concerns. Good thing too, because despite the fact that I thought my anxiety levels couldn't get any worse, over the past couple of weeks they've gone supernova. Yesterday, I had to choke back miserable, self-condemnatory tears when I left my five-quid, mini-compact umbrella on a bus. The day before, I experienced actual *physical* pangs of guilty stress about being two minutes late for the dental hygienist, when I was booked for most of the hour anyway. I never even used to know what 'pangs' really felt like before. The other day, I even caught myself worrying about hanging up on a PPI cold caller.

After I'd put her off brusquely and put the phone down, I visualized her sitting at her tiny, cramped workstation, locked into an enormous grid of other cold-caller workstations that stretches away into infinity. It's India, so it's infernally hot in there, and the fans have packed in. She's pretty and petite and innocent looking. She's sitting sweating in front of her huge target list, staring at a curling, sun-bleached photo of her many bright-eyed children, worrying whether she'll be able to feed them this month out of the tiny pittance she earns for a successful call. This is a new low. Not only have I succumbed to a ridiculous level of neurotic oversensitivity to pretty much everything – but my imagination has degraded so far that I'm incapable of conjuring up anything but the most patronizing and offensive of female stereotypes.

All I need, it seems, is one tiny nano-grain of concern with which to build a giant asteroid of guilt, self-doubt, panic and fear that hurtles through my mental solar system like... a giant asteroid of guilt, self-doubt, panic and fear. Maj has suggested evening primrose oil. My mum-in-law says she read in the paper that black cohosh is good. I say, are you kidding? That's like passing me a roll of budget paper towel and telling me to mop up the Atlantic Ocean.

I've got to do something, though. And soon. Because apart from anything else, I've started spotting how often I'm taking out my frustrations on S, along with my multiplying manias. I'm also avoiding people I normally like to spend time with or talking to. I'm doing a lot of displacement online surfing, searching for miscellaneous answers to mysterious questions such as 'do all Europe's eels *really* return to the Sargasso Sea to breed?' (my second step-mum once lost an antique desk in a bet over this); and 'where do you source the tiny rubber bands they use to castrate lambs with?' (my old friend, Sue, has a sheep farm and she was describing how they do castrating when I was up there last year).

To push back against the creeping paralysis of navel gazing, I've decided to try a bit harder with some kind of regular physical exercise. I could do with the endorphins, I tell myself. But there's no way I'm going to a gym to join 'spin sessions' with a load of jocks and jockettes suffering from steroid-induced, buff-body syndrome, so it's going to have to be swimming for me – 30 minutes minimum, at least every other day. It may bring me some inner peace. Or at least save my waist from going doughnut.

I arrive one Tuesday at the municipal pool, which, it turns out, is dead cheap for the over 50s. I should be pleased, but since I'm not 'myself,' I manage to find this incredibly depressing. I *don't want* the oldies concessionary rate. I don't want concessions made at all, not yet, anyway. I don't want to be 'supported' or 'encouraged' to keep fit either. I get so huffy about this while I'm filling out the forms that I even briefly contemplate paying full price, just so as not to be condescended to. *Really* losing it now, I chide myself.

Once I've pushed past this obstacle to my resolve, the pool turns out to be okay – a perfectly functional, modern basin of super-heated, over-chlorinated water with a couple of 'free-swim' lanes and a kiddies' pool alongside it. It's fifteen minutes' walk from my house so I can feel I'm really giving myself a work out – walk, swim, walk. I go there three days running. I quickly decide I don't much like the changing area, which is mixed, not all that clean and has tiny cubicles for changing in, so you keep banging your elbows on the sides of it as you try to get out of or into your gear. Relentless dance music, piped off the local radio, is blasted out all over the building, giving every corner of the place an unquiet, hectic ambience. It's also really busy in the pool, whether I go morning or afternoon, so it's hard to swim for more than a few yards at a time without stopping. And with my new goggles on, it's hard to avoid the odd, unpleasantly intimate view of a complete stranger's corn problem, or surgery scars, as they flap up the lane ahead of me.

The fourth morning in, I'm whining about this to S. I don't think I'll bother with the swimming any more, I tell him moodily. It's smelly and noisy in that pool, and the people aren't all that friendly. He suggests I could try out the university Olympic Pool, next door to where he does footy training on Thursday nights, but I'm very down on this suggestion. I imagine a huge, glassy sea of cold, blue water, full of streamlined swimmers in 'skin' swimming cozzies, silicon hats and nose clips, with kickboards and those strange polystyrene bones clamped between their thighs as they churn through the water like horizontal human wind turbines. Even the *thought* of an Olympic Pool is daunting. It's 50 metres long! I'm not sure I could swim all the way up it without an accompanying paramedic and an ambulance on standby.

But in fact, when I finally give in and go for a trial session, it's not like that at all. Arriving in the Ladies' changing room, I'm tense about the swim and a bit annoyed with myself for even thinking this was a good idea – but as I pull off my clothes in the clean, quiet, communal, benched area, I note from the easy chatter that I'm surrounded by a reassuringly friendly cross-section of the sisterhood (and a couple of very small naked boy children with tiny, stand-up penises that they can't stop holding onto, however much their mothers look embarrassed and scold them). Young and old, dark and light, tall and short, large and small – there's every shape and age and nationality of female – and from all backgrounds, not just from the student population, the uber-fit, or the leisured, middle class cohorts of self-satisfied self-improvers.

And the pool is… nice. The space is spotlessly clean, calm, naturally lit by a vast window that runs along one fifty metre side. The water is cool but not cold, crystal clear and it uses ultraviolet light as a filter as an alternative to an overdose of chlorine, which sounds reassuringly effective and high-tech. A small army of silent but smiley young pool guards seems to be on constant watching, scrubbing and polishing rotation, so the poolside area has a well-managed but easygoing feel. And there's enough room, enough lanes and enough variety of swimming styles and proficiencies that I can swim at the speed I want to, without annoying anyone faster, or risking having my nose rammed up anyone's bum.

After the first five minutes of breathless alarm – will that very young lad on his seat atop the guard-post have to dive in to save me as I drown in front of him? – I get into a sustainable stroke rhythm. Up for a breath and down for a stretch. Up for a breath, down for a stretch, up for a breath, down for a stretch…

Under the water it's quiet and pale blue, still and clear. Shafts of sunshine pierce the surface as I reach through them. I forget to be worried or annoyed or disappointed with myself as I chill out to the sound of bubbles jostling round my face when I exhale. I share a smile or two with other swimmers as we pass each other at the ends of the lane. I feel wobbly and shagged out after twenty minutes, but decide to push on for the thirty, then I think maybe I could make thirty five… I finally come out, a whole forty minutes later, desperate for a pee, but feeling like I've won Olympic Gold. Standing under a hot shower back in the changing area, I punch the air in triumph. I can do this! I can deal with this… get back in control. As relief and a sense of achievement wash through me, I well up with tears and have to turn my face to the tiled shower wall to avoid attracting attention.

On a high of endorphin-induced positive thinking, I buy myself a new cozzy from the sports shop, some extra-comfortable goggles and a high-fibre, low-cal lunch from M'n'S as a reward (expensive but I deserve it) and return home to work. Over the next few days, I find that if I don't swim, I feel the swift return of The Mad.

I go back – every day for a fortnight. And things start to change. My sleep improves a bit. My brain doesn't flatline quite so much. Anxiety subsides. My appetite alters: I don't hanker after quite so many biscuits and crisps as usual. I even decide to try staying off the alcoholic units during the week, as a way of reducing my calorie intake and feeling ready for the swim the next morning. I stabilise my daily fix in the pool to forty minutes, which I calculate means I'm managing more than a mile a day. I'm quietly amazing myself. And I'm discovering that feeling better about myself – managing to tick off these modest achievements – helps me keep a perspective on the other stuff. I tell S about it. He confirms that I look and seem better – brighter, healthier and happier, he says. I get on the scales at the pool. I've lost three pounds! I'm still prone to anxiety relapse, especially over the question of whether my new-found equilibrium can withstand any pressure, but I'm excited by this new me.

*

The following Monday, I have to get my swim in early because I've finally got the go ahead from the PR people at the Ministry of Defence. I'm going to be allowed to visit Colchester garrison, to interview and generally hang around with a group of gunbunnies. In contrast to the way I've been feeling about work recently, I'm actually looking forward to the day, so I'm in an unusually positive mood as I kiss S goodbye, walk down to the river through the leafy, peaceful Cathedral grounds, jump on the train and rattle down the London line as far as Colchester.

The only slight hitch in my bounce is delivered, a few minutes before we pull in at Colchester, by a sudden twinge and a sort of dragging, heavy feeling in my lower abdomen that almost certainly means I'm starting a period within a few hours. Jeez. Maybe it's just phantom twinges. At least I'm wearing black trousers. And with any luck it won't start until I'm on my way home. And anyway, I'll be with women the whole time so it won't be so bad if anything embarrassing happens. I head for the loos, nevertheless, and go for the full metal jacket approach to sanguinary safety – i.e. a mega absorbent sanitary towel *plus* a mega absorbent tampon. I check I've got plenty of replacements for both in my bag. And even spare knickers. Sorted.

Once accepted by security, and passed inside the barracks, I'm joined by a press liaison officer who I've already met during the vetting process at the MoD in Whitehall Place – an athletic-looking, well-spoken female Captain in her mid-thirties. She walks me across a broad, graveled area between the gate and the Regimental HQ – a low, rectangular Victorian building built of brick but largely covered in creeper.

She explains that I'm going to meet a young female lieutenant, along with a number of the gunners (privates), 'lance bombs' (lance corporals) and 'full screws' (corporals) who make up her battery. We go in by the main doors and head for the open lounge area opposite the Regimental Mess. The lounge is tired and old-fashioned but comfortable, dotted with sofas and easy chairs. We sit and await the arrival of the Brigadier General in charge of the gunbunnies, who I can't help imagining as a bluff, middle-aged, moustachioed toff.

As it turns out he's a tall, good-looking, 40-something, reassuringly unstuffy Aussie. He dismisses the press liaison officer, orders coffee and we settle at opposite ends of one of the sofas to chat. This isn't social, though. A series of this sort could turn out to be good for Army PR, or quite possibly, a threat to its image, security and morale. It's his job to assess me and my attitude to the series and the research. For my part, I'll never get access or good material if he doesn't trust me, so I have to try and reassure him that I'm not an idiot, and I've got no intention of seeking out salacious stories for their own sake, but without giving up the editorial control that the Army always wants over fictional depictions. I want to dramatise honest 'real life' experiences, I tell him, but I'm not interested in briefing out against the Army for the sake of it, or exploiting hard-working women doing what I imagine is a bloody difficult job.

Within fifteen minutes it's fairly clear he likes me. I get the impression that he might even be slightly attracted to me – a surprise, but not necessarily a disadvantage when you're doing research. He invites me to join him later for lunch in the Mess, then he hands me over to the female Lieutenant – Fizzy (short for Felicity) – who's going to show me round the life of a gunbunny.

Fizzy is ever so slightly chinless but open-faced, enthusiastic and honest, with a solid sense of humour. And the next couple of hours are really eye-opening, reminding me why I love my job. I get to indulge my innate nosiness to the max. First of all Fizzy shows me her own 'pad' while we discuss things like whether army girls find it easier to pull blokes than civilian women (answer: no, the opposite, so they generally lie about what they do). Next, she takes me to see where and how the female ranks live: in basic dormitories of up to six women a room. Then she sets me up with a bunch of young gunners for a Q and A, although they're entirely unused to being spontaneous around senior ranks, and they've clearly been warned by the liaison officer not to say anything controversial, so their answers to my questions are more than a bit bland.

We have coffee with a much more interesting Sergeant, who's a single mother about to return to a combat zone. But she's got a problem. Her parents had agreed to look after her children during her tour, but her mother's been taken seriously ill and there's now a chance that the children may be taken into care while she's away serving her country. I'm gobsmacked that this is even a possibility. Surely the Army will support her, look after her kids somehow? But the short answer is no, it won't. Wow. Fizzy announces it's time to show me what they actually do when they're 'in the field'.

We walk across a parade ground, past a bunch of pre-fab buildings, to a large hangar. There are workshops and offices built into one side of the hangar, but the main space is dominated by two AS90s, around which lots of soldiers are working. An AS90 is a self-propelled artillery piece, which basically means a big, tracked vehicle like a tank but with a massively oversized gun barrel stuck on the front. Fizzy commands one of these things, along with a mixed crew of five.

She invites me to climb into the gun. The operating space inside it is tiny – about a six feet square cube – and even that space is cramped because there's the targeting and control end of the massive barrel protruding into the middle of it, plus radio equipment, shells and other stuff I don't recognise. I'm told by one shy, young gunbunny that on active service, the crew of five has to *live inside* this box for days at a time.

"So how do you manage the male-female thing if you're stuck in one of these for a week in hostile territory – or even on Salisbury Plain?" I ask Fizzy once the gunbunny has moved on. "I mean, it's obvious there's zero privacy. Do you take tents with you or something?"

"No room in there to store tents," she points out with a smile.

I'm awestruck at this.

"But what about… if you're on or whatever," I ask, prompted by further unpleasant twinges in my lower abdomen.

"Like I said. You get on with it. The lads try to wind you up, call you a split-arse, make sure everyone within a mile of you knows it's rag week… or they might dig up your tampon and dump it in your brew or whatever… you just ignore it."

For a nano-second I'm imagining being handed a hot drink with my own used tampon sitting in it in place of the teabag, but luckily my mind goes into emergency shutdown.

The armour-piercing shells, which have to be loaded in, like everything else, through the door in the back of the monster machine, are hip high when stood on the floor, the width of an elephant's leg (a young one anyway) and weigh not much short of a hundred pounds. While Fizzy is showing me this enormous, bullet-shaped shell, one of her gunners (male) walks by, salutes her with an unpleasantly sly grin on his face, then challenges her to lift the shell.

"You can pick that up easy, can't you Ma'am," he comments snidely. "Show our visitor how tough you are".

I'm expecting Fizzy to tell the little shit to piss off, but instead she tilts her head, shoots him a quick grin and steps up to the challenge. The gunner raises his booted foot and kicks the nose of the shell towards her. Fizzy catches it expertly between her thighs as it falls, and in one clean movement she wraps both arms round the thick end and hauls it up and against her body, her pale, English-rose face reddening quickly with the effort.

The gunner puts his hands together in a brief, silent clap, then walks on. I'm outraged on Fizzy's behalf, but so impressed and delighted with her victory over her snidey, cocksure subordinate, that I nearly kiss her.

"Can't let that kind of thing go," she explains evenly as she lands the shell back at my feet with a breathless shrug and a grimace. "We have to keep our end up with the lads or we don't get the respect."

'That's incredible," I tell her. "How do you stay fit enough to do that – even once?"

"I don't really," she admits ruefully as we walk on towards her office. "Last month I popped both kneecaps, I'm only just back from rehab, so I'm trying to avoid too much heavy lifting."

My mouth has dropped open. "What do you mean 'popped both kneecaps'?"

"Happens if we carry too much weight, 'specially the girls. The kneecaps jump out of where they're s'posed to be, slide round the side. Bloody painful – I know people who've been crippled by it, or got hooked on morphine getting over it – it's not life threatening though."

Oh good, that's fine then... not.

"So, how many women in the Army suffer from popped kneecap?"

"Happens to quite a lot of us," she explains. "With the weights we carry – the Bergens..."

"Bergens?"

"Army issue rucksacks – fully packed they can weigh a hundred pounds or more... plus they're not designed for females – physiologically speaking – all the weight goes onto the thighs not the hips, so the bit that goes first tends to be the kneecaps."

I feel weak at the kneecaps.

"You okay? Want a break for a brew?" she asks kindly.

*

An hour later, I'm sitting at a great long, linen covered table in the paneled Mess Room, taking lunch with the Brigadier (it's just the two of us). Somewhat incongruously we are also being waited on by a huge, burly and heavily-braided mess attendant. The Brigadier is flirting with me in a non-threatening, easygoing kind of way. I'm relieved that, for now, at least, the temperature in the large empty room, combined with my sensible choice of clothes, means that I'm not having to sneakily dry my face every time he's not looking. All good.

But I'm still getting over the shock of the single mum Sergeant's predicament, and the physical challenges that Fizzy and the other women have told me about, and I'm feeling angry about it all on their behalf. And I've had a couple of glasses of wine. And my uterus has started cramping painfully. For all those reasons, I've temporarily parked my mission priority in being there.

"Couldn't they have Bergens specifically designed for them at least?" I'm asking, the tone mildly confrontational.

"Yes, they could – and they probably should. But this is the Army. Things move slowly. We do our best to keep them fit for the job. It's not in our interest to…"

I cut him off.

"If you're going to have women in the forces at all, surely there's no excuse for handicapping them like this."

"I wouldn't say we're handicapping them," the Brigadier answers evenly, but I've suddenly lost concentration. Something strange and unsettling is happening… inside me. It's not exactly painful, but there's movement – quite obvious, unmissable, significant, downward, internal movement – in my uterine region. I can feel myself getting very hot, very quickly.

"I, er… I'm sorry." I shove back my chair. "Could you excuse me a moment?"

He looks slightly thrown. "Yes… of course. Am I boring you?" he quips with a smile, trying to ease the sudden conversational caesura.

"No, not at all. I… won't be a minute…" I add unnecessarily.

I grab my bag and walk out of the Mess as slowly as I can, feeling his eyes on me as I go. Between my legs I can already feel blood breaching my underwear and soaking my trousers. Shit.

I cross the hall between the Mess Room and the lounge area as quickly as I can, but at the same time trying to keep my pelvic floor muscles clenched, and my legs as close together as possible. I feel dizzy. I reach the door to the Ladies' and push it open. With relief, I see it's empty. I rush into a cubicle, push the door closed behind me, undo my trousers and drag them down, squatting over the toilet as I do so. I feel the downward movement accelerate. As I steady myself with a hand on the wall and stare between my thighs into the toilet bowl, the water quickly darkens with thick splashes of blood… and I'm shocked to see myself giving birth to the ultra-absorbent tampon, swiftly followed by what looks like big chunks of blackcurrant jelly in blood sauce. Shit!

Ten minutes later, with the help of a whole toilet roll, a lot more sanitary protection and a messy and complicated change of knickers, I risk leaving the cubicle and checking myself out in the mirror. I look very pale and greasy-faced. I feel shaky and mildly traumatized. But that's not by any means the worst of it. So much blood has soaked into and around the crotch and backside of my trousers that, although it's invisible for now against the dark cloth, I know that I can't now risk sitting down on anything that's upholstered, especially if it's light-coloured material. I try to remember how the dining chairs are upholstered in the Mess but I can't bring them to mind. And I can't stay in the toilet for the rest of the afternoon…

I walk back through the lounge. I try to think myself back into my role as a confident, professional writer on a research trip. But instead I keep seeing the sequence in *The Shining* when the river of blood flows down the corridor and into the lift. I enter the Mess and look over quickly at the table and the chairs. They're covered in cream-coloured linen to match the tablecloth. OMG. I won't be able to sit down *at all*, unless I want to leave a massive bum print in menstrual blood on the seat opposite the Brigadier. He stands as I approach, fixing me with his easy smile.

"Okay?" he says, clearly not expecting it not to be.

Part of me would like to say no. Part of me would desperately like to point out my pallor to him, explain exactly what's just happened in all its grim, gory detail, and demand a hug and a taxi home NOW. But obviously I can't. Nor can I stand up for the rest of the meal.

"Yes, fine".

Arriving at the table with a fixed smile, I'm frantically scanning the vicinity, trying to come up with a solution to my predicament. I spot the large linen napkin I was given at the start of lunch scrunched up on the table next to my half-eaten, over-cooked roast pork. In what I hope is a deft and completely unnoticed movement, I grab it as I step forward of my chair, then release it *under* me onto the seat, just as I sit down.

As I pull myself in to the table, feeling covertly to make sure that the napkin is properly in place, my thinking is that with any luck, the blood sponged up by my trousers won't be enough to soak through the napkin to the chair seat, and that I'll be able to pick up the napkin stealthily when I'm leaving and stuff it into my bag for disposal later. The mess attendant will no doubt spot that it's gone when they come to clear up lunch: "That lady you were lunching with, Sir... I hate to point the finger but I think she might have half-inched one of our linen squares." Not a great impression to leave the Army with. But maybe not as bad as a signature semi-dried bum print in blood. I'm thinking all this as the Brigadier refills my wine glass.

"Oh, by the way, Fizzy suggested taking you out onto the assault course this afternoon for a taster. You up for that?"

*

On the train on the way back, I'm so exhausted I can hardly move. My head pounds, my stomach aches, I can't get warm and I'm feeling world-historically sorry for myself. The dried blood all over the crotch of my trousers has crisped the material sufficiently that it's rubbing my thighs. In my bag is the bloody, stolen square of linen – the Napkin of Shame. I can smell its pungent, irony whiff as I stare out of the window into the darkness, reliving the end of lunch and the long afternoon's trial. I'd firmly turned down a go on the assault course, obvs, but even so, I'd stopped being able to focus on anything I was hearing and seeing. I'd been forced back to the toilets several times as my body continued to eject what seemed like an impossible quantity of blood mixed with squidgy bits of jam and liver-like stuff.

At least I'd been able to explain to Fizzy about having a bad period – but every minute of the rest of the day, I just wanted to be back at home with a blanket, a skip full of ibuprofen, a never-ending pot of tea and hugs from S. I feel my throat tighten and swallow back self-pitying tears. If this is going to happen every other time I try and leave the house for work, we're going to starve... and I'm going to be under effective house arrest for... what... months? Years...?

I stop sniffling as the trolley appears in the carriage, expecting to see one of the several friendly ladies who normally drive it. But this one's new: nineteen or twenty, with a crap tattoo of a snake round her wrist, a badly home-baked head of bleached hair and a blank, bored look in her eyes. I stare at her coldly as she passes, horrifically jealous of her, despite all her obvious disadvantages. Why does *she* deserve to be young and menopause-free? I feel such a sudden spike of angry injustice that it triggers an instant creative thought: could I sell it as a story...? The desperate menopausal woman who thinks she can regain her youth by murdering someone under 21, and then maybe feasting on said youth's blood and remains, or taking over her identity, or... I really like the idea for about half a minute before sober judgement kicks back in.

Finally, we arrive and I'm walking out of Norwich station into the dark and (despite the season) an icy East wind, feeling like death not even warmed up. There's one cab waiting. I crawl into it and am about to tell the driver where to go, but he recognises me and remembers where I live.

"You been working up London again?" he asks chattily as we drive away. Norwich is a small and friendly enough place that it's not unusual for people to recognize each other like this.

"Not this time," I explain. "Colchester. Bit of a long day though," I tell him with a slight lump in my throat.

"Well you're alright now, love," the driver says with genuine care in his voice. "I'll have you back home in no time."

It's such a kindly, unasked for response that I feel tears of gratutude welling up.

"Thanks," is all I can manage to reply without blubbing.

The driver chats gently on about matters of local interest as we cruise through the city centre – a likely mid-week win at Carrow Road; a poor old gentleman taken seriously ill off the train earlier – and I get increasingly grateful and emotional and teary in the dark behind him. I want to kiss him when I get out. Instead I give him a massive tip.

I'm closing the front door behind me as S appears from his office.

"Good day, babe?"

I burst into floods of inarticulate tears. Whatever S really thinks about this, he wisely doesn't say. He wraps me up in a hug, and with the same genuine, kindly tone as the cab driver, suggests he can sort me out in two minutes with a nice, reassuring cup of tea.

***

8. THE RED ZONE (JUNE)

A couple of weeks later, I'm still haunted by The Colchester Experience. For the first few days afterwards, I was half expecting a call from the Brigadier's office to say that after all he wasn't sure he was happy to facilitate further research. But that hasn't happened, yet. In the meantime, I've been writing up my notes from the day, and working on a potential format, stories and characters for the series. But I can't stop drifting off and returning to the one subject that has now taken over every waking thought and quite a lot of my dreams. Me. And MMe. Specifically: what the hell will happen next? It appears I'm trapped on a hormonal rollercoaster that's in more or less constant danger of losing its grip on the tracks, but that I nevertheless can't stop or get off – that much is becoming crystal clear.

I can't help wondering again about all the other women who *must* be going through this very thing, and asking myself what they're doing, how they cope and why we aren't all talking to each other about it. What if you're unlucky enough to have a really high pressure, front-of-house kind of job? How would that work? What does Angela Merkel do if she gets stuck in the loo dealing with catastrophic leakage and a sudden inability to remember the phrase 'fiscal policy', when she's supposed to be in a G20 meeting, signing off world-altering fiscal policy? Who does she talk to? I wish I knew. I wish there was a helpline. And no taboo.

Why shouldn't we be able to explain to a male colleague or acquaintance that we're having a hot flush or a nasty period without them reacting as if you'd just shown them an HD download of your recent vaginoplasty. And in cases where the symptoms are bad enough to be beyond management, it would be brilliant to be able to apply for or declare a short *menopause sabbatical*, without totally blowing your credibility as a professional. Why not, if they give people parental and compassionate leave?

More than anything else, it would fundamentally transform my situation if I was able to have these conversations with a fellow sufferer. Maj is great, but she isn't going through it. Ditto Caroline, O's girlfriend, Lou, all my schoolmates, and every other female of my close acquaintance, as far as I can tell. S is trying his best but he hasn't got a clue what's happening to me. I desperately need someone who *gets what it really feels like to experience this.* But there's no one. In desperation, I decide to have a go at seeking virtual support. This time I ignore symptoms keywords and google menopause + blog + support – and wow! There are hundreds of them. I click hopefully on one called Menopause Madness, but what comes up, disappointingly, is a whole bunch of ads for things like incontinence pads and 'rejuvenair' fans. Jeez. I try another one. It tells me that it's time to 'honour my own knowing'. Begin with admitting I don't know… the way out is the way in… going down and in will lead you up and out. *Really*?

Unless the writer is suggesting that there's some kind of Tantric positioning that improves menopause symptoms, she's lost me right there... I click on another one and find a poem that starts with a sentiment I can relate to about feeling like you're being chipped away by the menopause, and it looks like it might even have an optimistic message about my life's mosaic coming back together, but then the poet hits the reader with the truth: that the pieces are held together by 'wrinkles and crinkles'. Not helping. I switch to a chat room, but all I get is a bizarre string about playing Scrabble to relieve the symptoms.

I want to scream. Whatever the magic bullet is that will cure me of my current afflictions, Scrabble isn't even on the longlist of possibilities. I have one last look through some posts and find one that offers me a French proverb: when a woman loses her blood she gains her voice. Well, I suppose I'm pleased for any sister who feels that way, but I *haven't* found my voice. Quite the opposite, in fact. I wander away from my laptop wishing I hadn't even looked at those posts. Five minutes ago I was feeling materially consoled by the notion that there might be, in fact there *was* someone, indeed hundreds of women out there who could understand and empathise – be on my wavelength. But all I've found is mad meno-bloggers and bad poets.

*

I haven't had the confidence to go back to swimming since The Colchester Experience – too scared to risk a repeat *Shining* while I'm in the pool. Actually that's not quite true, I risked going back once. My period had finally finished, although after the liver and blackcurrant jam phase, there were six or seven days of is-it-or-isn't-it-really-over to put up with. But I remembered how much better I'd felt in the water for those few weeks, so I thought I'd override my paranoia about flooding the pool with menstrual blood and make the effort.

I'd already spotted that there were busier and quieter times, so I go for the end of lunchtime, hoping to get a lane to myself and an opportunity to inject myself with some endorphin-induced calm and positivism. The changing room is very quiet. Good start. I haven't forgotten any of my swimming gear. Result. And the pool, although not empty, is reassuringly calm.

I'd been a bit worried that the gap would make a difference to my stamina, but again I'm pleasantly surprised. Two lengths in, I'm gasping a bit, but five later I've got a reasonable, solid rhythm going that not even a very splashy, middle aged male crawler can disrupt. All good. And then it lands. Or rather, *she* lands. A young woman crashes suddenly into me from the general swimming area next to my lane. As I disentangle myself from her and come up spluttering for air, I feel a little lava surge from my internal pop-up volcano.

"What the...?"

"Sorry" the young woman says. And smiles. The smile is broad and open. The girl is obviously from Southeast Asia. Obviously an overseas student. I notice another girl of about her age, and a boy just behind her. They've been playing in the water. I adjust my goggles.

"No problem," I manage magnanimously. I push off again, heading for deep water and the calming sound of bubbles. Up for a breath, down for a stretch... up for a breath, down for a stretch... the irritation slips away. I begin to think about characters for my group of fictional Army girls: how many, how to create strong personalities for them without falling for stereotypes, and what kind of written format to present them in...

As I turn and push off through the water back down the lane I see the bottom half of someone looking suspiciously like the girl who crashed into me. She has now entered my lane on *my* side, and is half swimming and half walking up it towards me. I try and ignore her, assuming she'll dip back under the divider rope before I reach her... but she doesn't... in fact she's now being joined by the other girl and they're standing chatting, blocking the lane completely. I'm still swimming but I can feel lava flowing up my middle. I stop in front of them.

"Hey, this lane is for lane-swimming only, you know." I point at the board at the far end of the lane that reads MEDIUM LANE with a graphic showing the anti-clockwise direction of travel swimmers should stick to. The girls frown. They turn to look at the board too. They both turn back to me, nodding and smiling widely.

"Yes. Sorry!"

"Okay." I manage to drop the frown, and even offer a brief smile before I lift the divider rope for them and encourage them back into the general swimming area. They're kinda sweet really. And at least they've got the message now.

I return to my rhythm and my characters. I'm particularly interested in developing a version of one of the gunners I met at the barracks who joined the Army at eighteen as an alternative to going to prison. She'd had a horrible life, been ignored and abused for most of her childhood and she was busy trying to blow up any chance of a future in the forces by repeatedly going AWOL with other peoples' stuff. She'd even spent a few months in the Glasshouse – the Army's 'correction centre'. Luckily for her, she was being mentored by... CRASH! Someone, and I can be pretty sure I know who it is, has just careered into me, causing me to choke on a large mouthful of water as I break surface. I tear off my goggles, confronting both girls, and their friend the boy.

"Sorry!!!" they pipe together, smiling.

I see red. I actually see myself *as a volcano*, with lava spewing out of my krakatoa head, pouring over my hair and flying off my arms, landing with a steamy hiss in the water around me. While I'm seeing this image of myself, I'm shouting at the two girls and the boy. I'm asking them what is so difficult about reading a sodding sign? I'm asking them why they seem to think it's perfectly okay to crash into me every two seconds, even though they AREN'T SUPPOSED TO BE IN MY LANE! Finally, before I even have time to think about thinking what I'm saying, I tell them that if 'they' can't read English or obey the rules, 'they' ought to go home to their own swimming pools.

This is terrible. Appalling. Unforgiveable. Anger turns to eye-watering embarrassment. I don't dare even look at them or at the expressions of other watching swimmers. I get straight out of the pool, mortified, and hurry to the anonymity of the showers. I can't believe what I've just said.

Racism is something I'd been made aware of at a young age. My mum spoke several European languages and got a job in the summer of '63, interpreting for the Ray Charles band, which was on tour in Europe. While they were in London, band members used to hang around at our flat in the daytimes before their gigs. I remember them as kings: beautifully dressed, gracious, demonstrative, noisy, generous, always laughing. But my Mum was also keen to educate us about the band's background: slavery in their families' past, segregation, oppression and the prevalence of prejudice in their present, and the potential of the Civil Rights movement for the future – so from that day onwards me and my sister regarded racists as the very worst scum of the earth. I had a fight with S once, because he slagged off a goalie in front of five year old O by calling him (the goalie) stupid and Scottish. I spent half an hour lecturing S on thin ends of wedges and my zero-tolerance policy towards othering.

So I hide in the showers for ten minutes, finally creep out, wriggle hurriedly into my clothes and rush home. I'm too horrified and embarrassed to even admit to S what I've done. I shut myself into my office and stare at my computer screen, wondering how I can make amends. But the bottom line is I can't. The Change has, apart from all its other horrors, turned me into one of the people I despise most in the world.

*

Yesterday, an unexpected package arrived in the post along with the free papers and pizza leaflets. It was from the daughter of one of my old school mates, just back from travelling in Japan. I opened it up to discover from the accompanying note that I was now the owner of a 'Japanese Menopause Fan'. It's beautifully made, in bamboo and fine, strong cloth, with a lovely design in sultry shades of blue that, at another time, I might have been very pleased with. But as I creep up to the wardrobe mirror (I've got a bad back from carrying too much shopping) and wave my new accessory uncertainly under my chin, wondering whether it's something I could use in public – say at a meeting or out for supper with friends – the overall impression is so unlovely that I make an on-the-spot resolution to turn down all social invitations for the foreseeable future.

I make myself some tea and slump into my chair. I feel exhausted. The energy needed just to maintain this white-knuckle ride on the hormonal rollercoaster is more than I can manage. I'm starting to find even doubting and hating myself too tiring to sustain. As I stare out at a patch of blue sky above me, I think: maybe it's time to do what S keeps suggesting, put the hair shirt in the wash and try a new 'reasons to be cheerful' approach. I decide to start by making a statement with some serious external sprucing – on me and the house – so I book a hair appointment, arrange a trip to the Garden Centre with Maj, have a very long talk with my friend and surrogate mum and adviser, Belinda (who unfortunately for me never menopaused because they removed her womb after her kids were born), and do an inventory of house issues that need addressing: a damp patch on the hall ceiling under the bath, a leaking kitchen sink, and carpets that were pearl grey and luxurious ten years ago, but are now looking matted and just grey.

Unluckily for me, there's only so much I can do to look better, if I'm *not* planning pregnancy, or the exsanguination of an eighteen year old, or having a whole box of Botox injections all in one go (and O, who's got a degree in biochemistry, says he'll never speak to me again if I'm stupid enough to ever inject myself with that poison). Luckily for the house, however, there's Billy. Having spent his whole working life on large-scale building projects, he's now semi-retired and content to tick over with a list of little jobs and a couple of short black coffees to keep him buzzing. He's friendly and cheery and efficient. He's not bothered about city-centre parking challenges. He's optimistic and great at finding solutions. All good.

A few days later, I've had my hair cut and highlighted, I've mulled over Belinda's wise and succinct words – "you're still young, darling, stop moaning" – I've hired a carpet cleaning machine, I'm due at the Garden

Centre with Maj in the afternoon and, as Billy arrives, I'm feeling, if not normal then at least a bit more organised and optimistic about life in general. Billy is in good spirits, we chat over coffee, then he gives me a short list of things I need to go and buy from the builders' merchants, a short drive away.

Because of my current tendency to lose stuff (or at least misplace stuff, or *think* it's lost) I subject the contents of my handbag to a serious audit before I leave to go to the shop. In particular I double re-check the location of my list, my glasses, my keys and the one debit card I'm risking taking with me, before slotting them back into their pre-selected pouches. I repeat the audit before I leave the house, and as soon as I get into the car. I'm boring myself stupid with these routines, but at least I'm reassured that I will be able to complete my task without incident.

I arrive at the builder's merchants and do the final prep. Hankies, check. Debit card, check. Keys, check. Glasses, check. List, check. The list I've got is short and straightforward: a large tube of silicone sealant, a large bottle of carpet cleaner, a set of new taps (not expensive), some ready-mixed polyfilla, a pot of white emulsion and a replacement halogen light plus bulb for the back garden.

Inside the shop, I spend ages looking at the various taps on offer and failing to decide which ones to get, even though they're barely different from one another. Then I get annoyed with myself for not even being able to choose a set of taps without dithering over them. Then I choose one, although I don't think I really like it, and get half way to the checkout before I change my mind. Then I experience what has become a horribly familiar double trigger: as my mind condemns me for being indecisive, the gun to my head of needing to make a decision causes adrenalin and heat to charge through my body, further dissolving any residual thinking power.

I hover sweatily near the taps for a minute while giving myself an irritable ticking off, put the taps back in my basket again and grab the rest of the items on my list in a rush, suddenly fixated on the fact that Billy's back home twiddling his thumbs and most likely blaming me for wasting his time. I hurry back to the counter and the shop assistant at the till – a balding, cardigan-wearing, slightly slovenly-looking man in his late 40s. At least there's no queue.

I pay, go back to the car, drop the stuff on the back seat, get in, then I decide to check to make doubly sure I've still got my card... and it's not in my bag. Shit. I look through my whole bag again, nothing. I look in the carrier bag with the taps in it, nothing. I look under my feet and around the car, nothing. I get out of the car and check it again, nothing. I check my jeans pockets, my jacket pockets, my bag again, the taps bag again, the car again, my pockets again, nothing. I want to scream and self-harm. But I tell myself to *think* instead. And I decide I must have left it on the counter in the shop.

I go back inside. I have to wait for a couple of minutes while the slovenly shop assistant serves a very young builder's apprentice in plasterers' overalls, who's questioning the amount of change he's been given. I examine the counter. No sign of my card. Maybe he, slovenly shop assistant, has spotted it and put it somewhere safe already. I have to dry my face with more than one tissue while I'm waiting because now I'm having a full-on anxiety-sweat. There's a second, slightly younger bloke also behind the counter, and I keep trying to catch his eye but he's doing something else with bits of paper and doesn't seem to want to stop to help me. I check the time. Every minute I'm standing here is costing me more of Billy's time and disapproval. Shit.

I castigate myself again silently for spending so long choosing the stupid taps. I castigate myself for being a dozy cow who forgets everything, wastes time and forgets her card. I silently curse the apprentice for being too innumerate to count his change properly. Finally, he's satisfied he's got the right money and walks out with his stuff. I step up quickly.

"I just paid for some things a minute ago and I think I must've left my debit card here, have you found it?"

The slovenly shop assistant looks at me with a bored expression. "No, Madam." The tone is mildly disparaging.

"I paid with the card and now I haven't got it, so I must have left it in here."

He shrugs, apparently barely interested. "Haven't seen it." That shrug. I conceive an instant violent dislike for him.

"Are you sure? You haven't looked yet."

"Not really anywhere to look, Madam." He gestures at the counter, which, it has to be said, is a small, clear space with nothing on it and nowhere much to hide a credit card.

"Maybe it slipped under the till or onto the floor."

He looks down at his feet for a nano-second and shakes his head. I look down too, searching the boarded floor on my side of the counter. I look at the till, but there's a kind of wooden beading that it sits behind, so the card couldn't really have gone under there. I notice the bloke who was too busy to help me a minute ago has now stopped what he's doing and is watching me with a patronizing expression of interest. I stare back at the floor and spot a small gap between the front of the counter and the floorboards. I bend over to stare at it.

"It could've slipped down there, maybe."

The shop assistant hesitates for a second, then bends over the counter to stare at where I'm pointing.

"Shouldn't think so."

"Have you got a torch so I can look?"

The shop assistant throws his eyes. He turns behind him and rifles in a plastic tray. He retrieves a small torch and hands it to me.

"Thanks," I say brusquely. I turn on the torch, whose battery is only offering enough power to create a yellow half-light, and squat down to point it at the gap.

"I think I can see something."

"There's not enough room under the…"

"I can see it!" I say forcefully. We need to get this board up."

"Can't do that."

"Why not? "

"Boss isn't here. I can't start taking the shop apart…"

"It's my debit card!"

Now the other bloke is leaning on his elbows on the counter, frankly observing this ditsy middle-aged woman getting worked up over her lost card. Enjoying it. I glare at them both. Suddenly I don't care if I'm the entertainment.

"I'm not leaving here without it."

The slovenly guy rolls his eyes again and slowly, reluctantly, edges out from around the counter. He takes the torch from my hand and squats down to look.

"That's not a card."

"How do you know unless we take the board up?" I press a tissue to my face again.

"I can see it isn't. It's like, probably a bit of paper or something."

Swallowing my pride but not my irritation, I rifle through my bag, find my glasses, put them on, and squat down to look again.

"I disagree. It's much thicker than paper. I think it's my card. You're gonna have to take up that board."

The shop assistant sighs audibly.

Belatedly I wonder if being polite will help. "Please." It comes out sounding pathetically pleading, but it works. Sort of. He says nothing. He wanders away back round the counter, as if there's a legal requirement for him to move in slow motion. He catches his colleague's eye with an irritable sneer. I hate him. In my mind I'm screaming at him: GET A BLOODY MOVE ON!! I check my mobile for the time again. Tick, tick, tick. He rifles in the plastic tray again and retrieves a claw hammer, watched by his mate. They exchange more looks. The slovenly one moves back round the counter, still in slo-mo. He squats back down and applies the claw to the end of the board. There's a ripping noise as the nails tear out of the wood. For some reason the noise calms me a little. He pulls it up. Lying on its edge against the side of the next door board is a business card of some sort. Shit!

"See?" he says with a smirk and a look that makes me want to grab the hammer out of his hand and embed it in his right eye socket.

With a brief, mumbled "Okay... sorry...", I hurry out of the shop and away from the humiliating stares of the two blokes. I try not to imagine what they're saying about me behind my back. I focus on the crisis at hand. Somehow, between the shop and the car, I've lost the card that accesses *our main account*. Did I drop it on the ground on my way out of the shop the first time and someone has picked it up? Sounds entirely possible. Why didn't I check the ground at my feet as I returned to the shop??? Stupid, stupid, stupid...

Then I remember the apprentice. He looked a bit shifty, now I come to think of it. Maybe he spotted the card on the ground as he came out and just walked off with it. Suddenly that seems the most obvious explanation. The innumerate youth has picked up my card, and instead of giving it back, he's hurried off to the centre of Norwich, which is, after all, one of Britain's top five shopping destinations, to spend ALL our remaining cash on massively expensive games consoles. Or no, wait a minute, he doesn't have my pin number, so he can't go shopping... except... of course! He's rushed straight back home, gathered his family round him, and they're busy loading their bottomless virtual shopping baskets with hugely expensive *online purchases*. Shit!

I get back into the car. I've got to get to my bank and stop the card, NOW. I haven't even got time to ring home and tell Billy what's happening. First, stop the card. Second, call home. I roar off through the traffic on my new mission, drive through a couple of yellow-to-red lights, and finally pull into a space outside my bank ten minutes later. I manage to scrape the wheel badly against the high kerb as I'm parking, but I don't care because I know what my priority is.

I rush into the bank.

I'm third in the queue.

Come on, COME ON! Every second is another online payment grabbed out of my account by that dishonest bastard of a kid, his family and quite probably all of his greedy teenage mates.

Finally it's my turn at the counter. I'm sweating like a vandalized garden sprinkler, but at least I've got an excuse.

"I think my debit card's been stolen and I need it stopped immediately," I blurt out to the young female cashier.

"Of course, Madam, I'm really sorry to hear that. I'll get it sorted out for you straight away."

I love this young woman. She doesn't argue. She's neat and tidy, not slovenly. She smiles instead of sneering. She responds positively. And not in slow-motion either. She takes my details and walks briskly away from the counter for a minute. I wait. She returns, pristine and pretty in her peach-coloured blouse and nicely done hair and makeup.

"Right, that's all done for you. Have you lost anything else?"

"No, thank goodness."

"Have you reported the theft to the police?"

"No, but I'm going there next."

"Good, well, I'm really sorry about what's happened. We'll get a new card issued for you straight away."

"Thanks so much, you've been great," I say sincerely.

I walk out of the bank, letting loose a huge groan of relief that provokes odd looks from customers on their way in. Right now I don't care, though. I've managed the crisis without a major incident and without drowning in a sea of my own angst and stupidity. I've pulled the iron out of the fire. I focus on my heart rate – it's going like a Pendolino – and decide I really need to calm down. At least from this moment on, that robber-apprentice and his hordes of thieving friends won't be able to get their hands on any more of our hard-earned cash. I get back to the car, open my bag to get out my car keys… and I can't find them. *Please* not again. I KNOW I put them in my bag before I went into the bank. I check my pockets. Nothing. I turn my bag upside down onto the ground. The keys fall out. Relief. Several two pound coins fall out. Bonus. Last thing out is my debit card. Shit! Shit! Shit! Shit! Shit!!!!!

That afternoon, after I've rushed back in to the peach-coloured cashier and admitted the card was in my bag all along, and she's told me that unfortunately it's too late, Madam, I'll have to destroy it immediately and await the arrival of the new one, I'm at the Garden Centre with Maj, asking her to give me one good reason why I shouldn't go and get myself sectioned or even put down humanely as soon as I've dropped off my ipomaeas.

"This whole situation *is* temporary, darling," she says. "Balance *will* return."

Her velvety voice is, as ever, balm for my spirits. It doesn't even really matter what she says to me half the time.

"That's what you've got to hang on to. It won't last forever."

"You're right." A trickle of relief.

"And quite possibly the worst is actually over."

"D'you think?"

I'm staring at a beautiful display of pelargoniums as I'm saying this and somehow just hearing Maj and looking at the pelargoniums is giving me hope.

"Someone I've been working with told me her menopause only lasted three months."

"Wow, really?"

"In the meantime, I was wondering whether… maybe you should take another stab at…"

I cut her off. "Not Gail and the upholstery virgins!" I plead pathetically. "Don't make me go back there!"

"Trust me," Maj intones. "The person I'm thinking of is definitely not a virgin."

***

9. LIQUID (JULY)

Maj is right. Rosalind's got five children and, at any given time, probably double the number of lovers. People naturally describe her as a goddess, because she's beautiful in a very glamazonian way – strong, muscular, sexy and somehow unknowable – and she has magic powers, though her cover is that she's a T'ai Chi teacher. I used to go to her classes when o was young, and Maj thinks I should return to her fold and get the benefit of some of her rebalancing magic. Maj has even offered to come along and do some T'ai Chi herself, to encourage me.

But for now I don't want to even look at anyone as gorgeous and brimming with vitality and balance as Rosalind. Without the swimming to therapise me, I'm finding it difficult to get out of bed again, let alone get balanced. The headaches are back with a vengeance. And I've missed a period entirely, so I'm carrying enough 'water weight' to rehydrate the Sinai. Although I had a few twinges a week ago, they've come to nothing. It's as if The Colchester Experience was a last throw of my menstrual dice. So has my procreative system now ground to a halt? Completely? Will I look and feel like a bloated python, forever?

Not for the first time, I wonder why I'm so depressed by the prospect of missing my monthly date with blood and pain. Asked to name one good thing about periods, nothing at all comes to mind. And although things have improved since the days when women were shut away to deal with menstruation and menopause in the dark because both were considered to cause 'debility' and madness, it's still one of those things that most females have to suffer in silence. I skype with Lou, my San Franciscan sister. I tell her how I'm feeling, at length. She reveals that she hasn't had a period for over a decade and can't imagine why I'd be feeling nostalgic about it.

"But doesn't that mean you must have gone through the menopause?" I ask, suddenly enthralled.

"I guess," she says. "But I was still in my 40s… too busy with work and life and the kids to notice."

Lucky for some.

Before she goes off Skype, Lou sends me a link to a viral U-tube video – to cheer me up she says. It's called 'Harden the Fuck Up, Australia' and it's an Aussie comedian who basically wanders round picking on sad characters and telling them to harden the fuck up. It's actually quite funny, though. And I get her point. I *should* be cheering up, because we're only a week or so away from getting off the rock and going to France, to the house that my Mum bought as a semi-ruin not long before she died. It's in a small, scruffy tourist town that sits on the edge of the Cevennes mountains, straddling the remains of a once huge but now depleted river, about fifty minutes' drive north of Montpellier.

The house is in the middle of the old town centre and it's what you'd call rough and ready, but we've been going for so many years, and we've shared so many good times with friends and family there, that it feels like home. This year we're going to get a whole month away, with quiet time to work and fun time to play with the friends we've made over the years, before more fun arrives in the form of an extended party for Anna's eighteenth birthday. On top of that, Lou is arriving from San Francisco to share in the celebrations, so I'll have my sister and my bestie with me.

I'm worried about how I'm going to cope with the heat, though. There's no air-con at the house, or even a ceiling fan, although it stays relatively cool inside because the walls are made of three-feet-thick stone. Normally I like heat, but I'm not sure what the combined effects of French *chaleur* and my own internal combustion will be. Maybe I'll overheat and explode, like a car engine. The thought sets up a whole new panic cycle. Could I actually die from a hot flush? I rush to my desk and google: "can you die from a hot flush?" It tells me that no one has been known to die from one, but suggests that hot flushes can be dangerous, and that's it's advisable to sit down and rest after you've had one, maybe even take a few days off work, until *you feel better*.

Who writes this stuff? If I took days off work after every hot flush, I'd never get to my desk again. Sit down until you're feeling better? Better than what? What do you do if you're getting one every five minutes? I decide to ask my phone-a-friend science consultant instead. O says I've got nothing to worry about. My internal temperature isn't actually varying very much, despite how it feels – it's just my bodily thermostat that's shot. As long as I do what I'd normally do to keep cool, he tells me, I shouldn't have a problem. Phew.

But these days, I can turn almost anything into a medical neurosis. Instead of organising myself for departure, I'm mooching round the house, morbidly tracking through all the grim health scenarios to come. Even if I get on top of this menopause stuff, I say to myself, even if I get out the other end alive, all that then happens is that I'm in Death's waiting room without my hormonal armour. I return to haunt the self-scare diagnosis sites on the internet. Like an addict, I've lost all ability to moderate my behaviour – I read up on itises that I don't dare discuss with S for fear of inviting chuckling dismissiveness, which, I've realised, tends to trigger even more certainty that I'm about to suffer a fatal episode of whatever-it-is-itis. According to wiki answers, the menopause itself can last a decade or more. It also tells me that I have to go a minimum of a whole year without a period *at all* before I can say that I'm *post*-menopausal, although that doesn't mean the symptoms will definitely be over with. The good news just keeps on coming…

Meanwhile, Menopause Me continues to evolve, and not in a good way. In the past I've been seen as someone with balanced views, but all that's over with now. The grey areas have gone. I'm living in sharp monochrome. As a result, *every time* my emotions are engaged by something small or large, I'm likely to feel tears or screams rising too. On top of that, the list of things that I disapprove of, dislike or even hate, is growing daily. The other day I sneered so unpleasantly and loudly to S about the lack of braincells of the girl behind the counter at the greengrocer's stall that he felt it necessary to jump to her defence.

"Ease off the bile, sugar," he implored me. "You don't *have* to have a PhD to weigh out kohl rabi."

I harrumphed, and backed up my position by criticizing her dress sense. These days, I'm horrible as well as useless, ugly and a racist. My bodily outflowings, whether sweat or blood, or mental or verbal bile, have become extreme as well as completely unpredictable. S says that it's not that bad, and that, a bit like the way anorexics stare in the mirror and see a fat girl, I'm seeing a serpent-headed harpie that isn't really there. But I think he's lying to avoid becoming a target.

And that's the other problem. In a real sense, S is trapped on the rollercoaster with me. Everything that happens to me, impacts on him too. And even his very buoyant reserves of empathy are depleting in the face of my meno-mania. He's started doubting me in ways that were never in question before. I can see it in his eyes. Is she *ever* going to get 'back to normal' again? Is she actually going to slap that girl at the greengrocer's, or decapitate the postman with her garden loppers the next time he dares to leave his rubber bands littering the doorstep? He looks at me sometimes as if he's wondering whether I did, after all, get abducted by aliens and replaced with a poorly achieved lookalike. And the fact is that's more or less what's happened. The real me dropped off an edge, shortly after buying the second most expensive sweater ever made, and doesn't appear to be coming back. Not for years. Maybe not ever.

*

One Friday morning, after a lot of miserable rifling through summer clothes that I don't any longer feel confident to wear, obsessive list-making (I'm bound to forget *everything* crucial) and querulous, cup-half-empty comments to S about the stress of leaving home for this long, we're packed and waiting for a taxi to take us to the station when I remember my Japanese Menopause Fan. It might come in handy to have it, especially if the two battery-powered ones I'm bringing with me run out of juice. I grab it out of a drawer, shove it in my bag and we're off.

I used to love flying when I was a kid. Or more accurately, my Mum loved it so much that her enthusiasm rubbed off on both me and Caroline for years. Back in the twentieth century, it was something novel, luxurious, only experienced by the few. In 1966, my Mum had just married her second husband, a Canadian who worked at Harvard, and we were off to live in Cambridge, Massachusetts. The prospect of a transatlantic flight on a BOAC VC10 felt like sci-fi – we were emigrating to the moon.

And the reality was barely less exciting. Once settled on board the sleek, supersonic bullet, we were given miniature models of the aircraft and shown movies that we listened to through our own individual headphones; we were also given eye masks, slippers and miniature pillows for sleep; and we were taken up to the cockpit by the stewardess, and got to exchange a few words with the pilot and crew, and stare open-mouthed at the banks of hi-tech controls in front of them, as we cruised over a huge expanse of ocean.

Living in the US was even more exotic and alien. Even though we'd come from a rented flat on the King's Road – Chelsea's cradle of the Swinging Sixties – everything 'over there' was sumptuous, modern and plentiful in comparison with mid-60s Britain. Our King's Road basement flat was dark, damp, cramped and permanently dripping with paraffin-stove vapour. Hot water was supplied, but only in tiny and unreliable quantities through a wall-mounted 'Ascot' heater with an open flame burning inside it that intermittently gave out or exploded. We didn't even have a fridge, just a dank larder cupboard with a draughty hole in the wall plugged with an ancient, dust-encrusted wire screen. In contrast, our American apartment had central heating, two bathrooms, unlimited hot water, colour television, a proper big, separate shower and a fridge the size of a one-bed council flat, filled with oddities and luxuries we'd never even seen before, like yoghurt, T-bone steaks and Sara Lee cheesecake.

The town of Cambridge, when we arrived in October, was so prettily decked out in autumn-red maples that it seemed to us as if we were living on a film set. We were enrolled at a progressive, newly-built school with a self-service cafeteria and whole walls made of glass where they taught us cool subjects like Debating and Oceanography. For some activities we were even integrated with children with severe learning and physical disabilities, who were also, progressively, taught in mainstream school. This was all in yet more contrast to our dark, satanic Victorian primary school, where disabled kids were called 'spazzes' and the most fun we ever had in class was gluing precut, pre-licked lengths of coloured paper into chains at Christmas until our tongues went tacky and we all felt sick.

While we were in the US we saw Americans land on the moon on the televisions we had *in every classroom*. We also went out with our first ever boyfriends: Caroline's was a funny, wild but charismatic Irish-American redhead; mine was a warm, funny, wise African-American thirteen year old, with a famous West Coast music producer Dad who used to send him white label LPs every week. We learned to love The Mothers of Invention, Country Joe, digging clams at the beach, skateboarding, pulling taffy (toffee), all-day baseball games at Fenway Park and playing Spin-The-Bottle, all of which made us seem pretty exotic to our mates when we came home to the UK for summer holidays. Caroline and I quickly learned to look forward to those unaccompanied flights back across the Atlantic, being treated like mini movie stars by kind stewardesses. It was cooler than cool.

But that was then. In the intervening years and especially since the arrival of the 'no frills' flight, I've enjoyed flying less and less. It's cramped and tense, and whereas I used to happily entrust my life to father-figure, ever-so-RAF Captain Thompson and his crew, now I'm not at all prepared to commit. The kiddies who work for Rubbishair are only just of child-bearing age, and some of them hardly know how to add up the money for the coffee, let alone fly an A380.

Anyway, in my current state of mind, I'm straight back on the terror-train if I have to get into a lift with a view, let alone strap myself into a metal cigar painted up to look like a cheap bus, and sit quietly while it hurtles down a runway and throws itself into the air in a ludicrous attempt to defy commonsense.

So we're on the metal cigar, and I've got eyes everywhere, analysing the cabin crews' dispositions (are they too tired to bother closing the doors properly?), watching the airside workers refueling below us (are there leaks; are they putting enough in?), and closely observing passengers as they pile onto the plane in case they are a) terrorists and/ or b) uncooperative or stupid people who won't turn off their electronic devices.

"What *is* that bloke doing rummaging in his bag?" I ask S, pointing.

"Looking for something, probably," he says, trying but failing not to sound a bit irritable.

I disagree, though. I think this bloke is very, very suspicious. I think the cabin staff ought to be noticing. But does that bored, fed-up looking flight attendant even care as she pounds along the central gangway clicking us off with her head-counter gismo?

"Probably not", says S. "She's only being paid about twenty quid for working this flight." Jeez.

Despite being surrounded by bomb-laden extremists and putting ourselves in the hands of grumpy, over-stretched slaves, the flight itself is just about okay and only a couple of hours later we walk out of Montpellier airport into the azure blue to be greeted by waving palm trees. I can't help unclenching as we drag our bags over the road towards the hire car office and the heat equalises my inner and outer temperatures in seconds. I glance at S. We're so lucky to have this chance to escape – to have somewhere to go that's full of good memories, good friends, and the healing warmth of the Mediterranean. We grin at each other – a real, shared, happy grin – the first in ages. I feel tears welling up.

"We're back," says S. "Everything's gonna be great."

"I know," I say as he hugs me hard. And then, as the thought occurs: "As long as we don't die on the A9 before we even make it to the house…"

Although we've only just arrived, we've got a big date for the next day. Our friend Etienne, who originally comes from Paris but settled in the town years ago, is, among other things, a keen participator in local politics and community life. And tomorrow is the annual 'Course des Radeaux', a raft race run down the river by a bunch of about thirty or more crazy locals, with a stop half way (just after the rapids) for a serious picnic. There are strict rules laying down the design and build of the rafts, all of which must be entirely homemade and can't incorporate any items already designed specifically to float on water. Versions in past years have included upended golfing umbrellas, floating bathtubs (only it didn't) and a canoe made out of an irrigation pipe.

Etienne's design this year is classic (he's already emailed us pictures) – a more or less conventional raft, all made out of the chunky bamboo that grows like a giant weed all along the river's edge. But Etienne has added some customized touches, including a hammock and parasol, and a small but fully functioning bar, complete with optics for spirits, which he intends to use to ply his rivals with drink on the way down the course, thereby ensuring their inebriation and his easy victory. Of course, this is a plan destined to fall flat because, obviously, he'll drink more than anyone else, fall in the river a lot and lose... But it's still a great raft, and a great day out, and S has happily agreed to join Etienne and his son as deputy barman and navigator. I'm way too panic-prone to go on the raft itself, so I'll focus on the picnic and the photo taking, in the company of other landlubbing camp followers and kids who walk the course along the river's southern bank, following the intrepid raftriders.

Having failed to either forget or lose the keys (result!) and opened up the house without mishap, we drop the bags, have a quick cuppa and make a bed, then S and I, still full of the joys of being back in the South, head over to Etienne's place for supper and an important pre-race conflab. Various of our other mates are already gathered there and we're soon installed on Etienne's roof terrace, trying to get our French working again while we drink local wine and munch pre-dinner nibbles. It should be paradise...

But it's about 35 degrees on the terrace, even at seven in the evening, and I quickly develop a Nile delta of sweat that begins to plough ever-widening courses over my face and body... even my ankles start sweating. I feel like I might actually be turning liquid – melting into a salty, sticky and slightly sour-smelling puddle. Even worse than the physical discomfort though, is the impact on my overall 'sense of well-being'. Within minutes I've gone from perfectly happy to tense, fidgety and irritable. I feel awash with hormones, like someone's slipped a mind-altering substance into my tapenade-on-toast. My French friends are kind, sympathizing with me about having 'les vapeurs', and one even produces a red plastic fan that I can use (I've left mine at home). But their sympathy has only got limited power to console. My clothes are wet through, my mood has gone dark and I'm desperate to get away, at least to shower and change. But Etienne's lighting up his barbecue to grill lamb chops... the temperature on the terrace rises another few degrees....

Then there's the smoking. How I can have failed to anticipate this further challenge to my equilibrium is beyond my reckoning. But it hadn't even occurred to me to wonder how difficult it would be *not* to smoke in France. Whereas all social gatherings in England these days are non-smoking – the one or two remaining hapless addicts will invariably be forced outside on sulky detention to perpetrate their anti-social habit in the wind and rain – the exact opposite is true in France.

There, despite a ban on smoking in public places such as restaurants, it's still more or less illegal *not* to smoke. Pregnant women, the elderly, the young, teachers, parents, doctors and nurses, the mayor, the cops... *everyone* smokes, all the time, and in a guilt-free, I'm-really-loving-it manner. The net result of this is that while I'm failing to concentrate on the local politics being discussed round the table, my eyes are glued to one, then the next, then the next friend, all chuffing away happily on their roll ups.

I can't take the strain on my resolve. Something snaps. I grab the fag suddenly out of S's fingers and take a long, deep lungful of smoke. And another. And one more. My head spins... my vision goes a bit sparkly round the edges... I feel sick and woozy... Bliss! In that two or three seconds, before guilt and disappointment at myself land as heavily as a no-frills flight in the hands of a Rubbishair trainee pilot, I revel in the self-indulgence of the moment. But it doesn't last. It's swiftly followed by another flamethrower of heat and a slug of overall mind and body discomfort that crank me spontaneously to my feet. Suddenly, I have to go.

I tell S and Etienne that I need to pop home and rush out. I run down the narrow alleyway that separates our two houses, between high, sheer, stone walls that keep out the sun even in high summer, and crash in through our front door. The sudden cool makes me shiver. I tear off my sodden clothes as I rush upstairs.

I collapse into the shower, where I wilt pathetically, blubbing under a cascade of lukewarm water. I feel insane with heat, sweat, confusion, guilt, fury and misery. I can't live in liquid form for one more day. I can't handle being so detached from the rest of un-menopausal life, struggling with all this. I definitely can't handle staying one more day in France if I've got to change my clothes every five minutes and sit and watch people enjoying themselves smoking all day and bloody night! The shower goes cold because the tank hasn't had time to heat up. I get out, but I can't face going back to the party. Instead, I crawl into bed under the eye of a tiny bat who's flown in through the open shutters and glued himself to the wall, and wallow in my own homemade ocean of sweat and self-pity until I fall asleep.

Twelve hours sleep later, the rollercoaster has passed terminal velocity, hit the bottom of the curve and is ploughing heavily back up hill, giving me a brief window of partial sanity within which, if I'm not going to insist we go home so I can sulk in the dark for the whole summer, I can try to strategise a French modus vivendi. S is sympathetic – and very keen not to abandon our plans and commitments – so he installs me on our (for now) cool, shady balcony for the morning. I stare down at the townspeople walking by to buy their bread and papers or deliver their kids to school, and ponder ways to stave off heat-induced mania. I open a notebook and write SWIM in the middle of the page and circle it. Other than standing in a cool shower 24/7, swimming is the only thing I can do that doesn't make me sweat, and helps me to maintain some kind of mental as well as physical balance. We haven't got room for a pool at our house – we haven't even got a garden, just a long balcony and a small roof terrace. But we've got friends with pools, and there's a generous couple at the local campsite who don't mind us using theirs out of high season, so I make the decision to use the cooler hours of the morning to work, followed by an early afternoon swim, followed by a few late afternoon hours chilling out on the roof terrace.

I launch the plan, but early results are disappointing. For the first few days the sheer volume of sweat I'm producing if I'm not fully immersed in cool water drives me beyond distraction. Sleeping is only possible in small bursts, not least because of the noise of the huge aircraft-engine-come-fan I've bought, whirring constantly at my side. Cooking is also proving difficult, because it turbo charges my internal combustion, and I really can't face putting food in front of us that I know I've sweated into.

In fact, trying to cook supper without inadvertently adding copious quantities of my own salty liquor to the chopped onions has already proved impossible. Instead, unless S is willing to make us his French Standard Supper of goat's cheese-stuffed-peppers, and I am prepared to eat it every night, we will go out to one of the inexpensive restos in the town. This will involve a significant added cost but since survival is my object, I'm ignoring the financial implications for now. And all the restos have open terraces where, as long as I've remembered my Japanese Menopause Fan, I can keep myself on the right side of raving bonkers.

Since we got here, I've become totally JMF dependent. I've realized that, unlike the little battery fans that are tiring to hold up and have the added disadvantage that they make the noise of a wasp buzzing constantly round your face, my JMF is silent, surprisingly effective and can even look quite elegant when properly deployed. I'd never noticed before, but now I'm looking, I spot how many natives in the south of France use one in summer. There's one flame-haired, middle-aged woman who I've had a bit of a crush on for years, who lives in a flat above one of the cafés in the town centre. Every morning, she sits drinking her *p'tit noir*, reading her paper and fanning herself beautifully. We always smile and nod and mouth 'bonjour' to each other, but now, when I arrive to do the same, we also share the pleasure of the fan. It's kind of comforting.

A week in, the signs are more positive. To start with, I've finally slowed down to Mediterranean pace. I've stopped trotting everywhere with a shoulder-hunched, stressed out, 'can't-you-see-I'm-busy' expression, and started ambling to and from the shops or the market or the café, stopping to chat with people I know, or telling myself that five minutes here or there doesn't matter that much.

I've also been getting up at dawn to help a friend do some planting on his riverside municipal allotment, and I've fallen head over heels in love with the place and its riot of flowers and edible jewels – my favourite being the bed of fat, baby aubergines hanging heavily off their stems like polished black sapphires. Walking through town in the quiet, balmy cool of the new day to spend a couple of hours with my hands in the earth is working for me like a daily meditation. And I'm even rediscovering the positive aspects of heat. Although it's extreme, at least I'm not forced to deal with the inversion effect. There are no cycles of hot, followed by freezing cold. There's just the one mode, day and night. Comfortable enough in a permanent uniform of shorts and T shirts, I'm liberated from the hassle of clothes altogether, and for now I'm like everyone else – hot and sweaty much of the time. I've also been reflecting on the fact that it's heat that has been the key to the town's restorative effect on me in the past.

Heat defines much more than just what you wear, when you're in the south. It's a condescending cliché regularly trotted out by Brits that people from the Mediterranean countries have a different 'attitude to life' – and it's true – but most of the differences are positive ones. Living in a sun-drenched, vivid, abundant environment promotes a special kind of openness, confidence and contentment in people, and as the days pass, I can feel the healing warmth of both seeping into me. Late afternoons reading on the roof, watching the buzzards circling the high rocky bluff that looms over the town, I let the sun and the sleepy sounds of life lived easily slow me to a complete stop, blasting away any and all coherent thoughts, to leave me in a dreamy, reflective state. And now that I've got an inner as well as outer blast furnace, this dreamy effect is more intense than ever. That, combined with the burnishing, blinding light and the contrasting cool comfort of the water when I swim makes me feel quite high. Liquid, light and heat is everywhere – inside and outside. But giving myself up to the sensory experience of these elements is oddly making me feel better, calming me down in a way I really hadn't expected. That and the aromatherapy massage sessions I've been getting from my friend Amanda. And the rosé. I'm smiling again. I'm thinking more positively again. And I'm sticking close (literally) to S again – both of us sweaty but happy together, for the first time in months. As the days pass, as long as I've got my JMF and access to a pool, I can relax and even enjoy.

I can look forward again too, to the imminent gathering of friends and family for Anna's birthday. Anna is already here, along with six of her best buds from school, all of them female, and all of them, like Anna, unfeasibly attractive young Beauties with extra-long legs, flowing hair and sweet smiles. S and I have decamped from the house for a week to let The Beauties use it exclusively as their party pad, and we've rented a gite with a pool nearby so we can work and play in comfort, and The Beauties and other arrivals have got somewhere to swim, before the main group of revellers turns up to occupy their own gite, also nearby.

The first time The Beauties come to our gite to swim, they decide to walk from town – a distance of only about two miles – but because they're not exactly getting up early, they finally set off in the broiling heat of midday. By the time they arrive, therefore, they're hot and pink, and they've already stripped off any clothes that they can risk removing without breaking the law and causing a multiple pile up on the road. So they're down to bikini tops and shorts so short they make a bikini bottom look modest. The teenage son of the gite owner, who does daily pool cleaning and maintenance in the garden, is busyish at work when the Beauties arrive, looking like they've just stepped off the set of America's

Top Model.

S and I happen to be watching from our terrace as the young lad, about sixteen, looks up lazily as he hears the electric gates swing open about fifty yards from where he's working. As he focuses on the Beauties, wandering in chatting and laughing, and they notice him, he first of all drops his jaw, then the hose in his hand, then, for reasons he probably doesn't understand himself, he runs for cover behind the pool house bushes. The Beauties think this is hilarious. And now the kid is stuck there. He can't come out without attracting more unwanted attention from the Beauties, so until we call them off to come and get a cold drink, he's got no choice but to lurk in a cruel, shadeless trap of his own making, while The Beauties giggle and make more gentle fun of him from the shade of the poolside pergola.

Later, while they swim and sunbathe round the pool, I'm s'posed to be working, but actually I'm thinking about youth and beauty, and that annoying conversation I had at my sister's house with Anna's ex. Do I *really, truly* miss being that age? Having everything ahead of me? Of course I do, I say to myself. Who wouldn't want to turn the clocks back… except… well… actually, amazingly, when I really think about it, as things stand, maybe I'm going off age-envy. I had a fantastic time being eighteen. But right now, with my friends and family around, no stress, a bit of a suntan, my menopause fan and my loving man, I don't want to change anything, or turn anything back. In this moment, right now, I'm content – at peace with what is.

***

10. SOL, SEX ET LUMIERE (AUGUST)

A week later, we've had Anna's big birthday bash along with several pre- and post-parties, just about got over the hangover, and now it's time for me and Lou to get back on a flight to London, where we're due to be meeting up for a camping weekend with a bunch of old mates. I'm still feeling pretty good. I've also had a call about a script-doctoring job on a feature length crime drama, so there's the reassurance that I'll have paid work to be getting on with as soon as we're back home. I'm even feeling energised enough to leave S, Caroline and the rest of the gang to soak up some more Mediterranean summer, while me and Lou brave a return to the English version to do some turning back the clock of a slightly different kind.

It's called The Summer of Love Party, and it's an annual, two-day retro psychedelic music festival, held each year in the grounds of a miniature but magnificent Tudor manor house in Kent. It's a small affair – probably no more than three hundred (mostly middle-aged) people camping in a large, gently sloping field – and most of the performers are tribute players rather than the originals (for obvious age-related reasons) but it's a great party if you happen to like that kind of thing, and a chance to catch up with people I don't see otherwise.

Contemplating living without my new soma – heat, light and swimming – is anxious-making, and there's the period problem – will I go into blood-tide mode while living on a field in the (probably) rain with only two or three shared portaloos? – but Lou is pragmatically reassuring. It's a weekend party with great mates – what could possibly go wrong? Most of the necessary equipment (tent, sleeping bags, waterproofs, industrial quantities of tampax) is being brought by our glam-camper bestie, Aggs, so our luggage consists of as much rosé as we can get in one big, shared hold bag, our toothbrushes, a change of clothes or two, my sine qua non JMF and Lou's equally precious, remote-control hearing aids (because she has a serious hearing problem caused by an accident at work several years ago).

We arrive at Montpellier airport in stinking levels of heat, to discover that the air-con has stopped working in the departure lounge, so walking in feels a bit like shutting yourself into a pre-set pottery oven. No probs though. I'm a heat specialist these days. I've got bottled water, loads of tissues and my JMF. What *is* a prob are the two incredibly noisy and spoilt little English kids – a boy and a girl – who are careering round the hall, demanding things, bumping into people and then breaking out into theatrical levels of wailing, while occasionally being shushed with a maddening lack of efficacy by their uptight-looking, hapless mother. She's in her mid 40s and she's sitting at the far end of our bench, in pink shirt and white jeans that are getting grubbier each time one of her brats gets up off the floor and launches itself at her with sticky fingers full of melted chocolate, or worse.

I am NOT sympathetic. Why can't she control these horrible little creatures? I'm reminded of S's (fairly harsh) view that parents should have to qualify for a license to breed. His argument is that if they make adoptive parents go through endless examinations and suitability tests, why shouldn't *all* parents. It's a hard one to counter, I tell Lou, as I lounge on the bench next to her, waving my fan under my neck smugly, and telling her even more smugly how brilliant O was when of the same age: how we travelled through many an airport without a second's fuss, while he angelically read a book, or asked me questions that I couldn't quite answer about the physics of flight.

Then I notice that I'm being eyed-up by the mother. In fact, she's staring at me fixedly. I notice she's got sweat beads all round her forehead, cheeks and nose and a full-on rivulet of the stuff running down either side of her neck. Her pink shirt is showing significant underarm staining. She's clutching what looks like the sodden remnants of her last paper hankie. I realise with a start that she's quite possibly more than just hot, and feel a modicum of sympathy for someone who's dealing with critical oestrogen depletion *and* young children. Poor cow.

She's still eyeballing me, though. I wonder why. Has she heard me griping about her and her kids to Lou? I doubt it. It's slightly irritating, because every time I look round, she's staring. Hard. I'm about to get indignant about it, then the penny drops. It's not me. It's my fan she's staring at. And the look is pure envy. I ignore her for a while. But every time I look back, she's watching me with the face of a drought victim who's been tied to a chair in front of a TV showing endless Evian ads. Finally, even I can't keep up the smug, hard bitch act. I slide along the bench towards her.

"You look like you're melting. Do you want to borrow my fan?"

She stares at me for a second with boggle-eyed surprise, as if I'd just offered her free family membership to the Soho Club in perpetuity and a guarantee that her kids would never EVER have to go to a state school.

"Oh gosh, could I?"

Before I can answer, she grabs the fan and throws her head back against the seat, swishing furiously under her chin as she'd seen me do. She lets out a sigh of relief so profound, I actually feel bad about judging her. But while I'm feeling bad, I'm becoming aware of something else in the now fairly busy departure lounge. It's a low, slightly animal, moaning sound. It's strange... I ask Lou if she knows what it is. She gestures with her flick of her head behind her. There's a woman a few benches away, and a man with her.

The woman's moans are turning to sobs. In fact, she's now crying her eyes out. Must be a bereavement, I guess immediately (because this has happened to me – when my Dad died suddenly, while S and I were on holiday in Spain). Or... she's just found out she's got cancer or something. Lou and I look sympathetically over at the man with her, who's doing everything he can to comfort her. Tough. Then the flight is called. For some reason this seems to trigger a new crescendo to the woman's tears. She moans out loud and sobs even more intensely. Sad... but a tiny bit weird too.

I'm still sympathetic but slightly put out, as Lou and I are buckling up on the plane, to discover that the sobbing woman and her bloke have slipped into the seats immediately behind us. My sympathy reservoirs are still on low and most of my menopausal stock of concern is reserved for me, myself, I. Lou gets this. She suggests we move to different seats, but in fact it's already too late because the plane is filling up and there are knots of passengers up and down the corridor trying to get stuff into the cabin lockers and settle their children down. Hey ho. We agree in whispers that sobbing woman will probably run out of steam and quiet down as soon as we get going.

No such luck. Instead, for reasons that quickly become obvious, the moment the pilot unlocks the ground brakes, the woman's sobs crescendo again. Everyone in the plane turns towards us as the aircraft begins to reverse away from the stand and the woman's cries get louder. Lou and I frown at each other. The woman calms down a little as a stewardess appears and has a hurried, whispered conversation with the woman and her escort, then returns to her jump seat for take off. But by the time we're picking up speed on the runway, the woman's cries are so loud that almost everyone, including all the cabin crew, are now watching her with concern, and some of the other passengers, especially the children, are getting anxious, restless and fidgety. A few passengers are looking angry, craning their necks towards the cabin crew, looking like they might actually disobey the warning lights, get out of their seats and try and smother sobbing woman with their in-flight mini-pillow. The woman is clearly terrified of flying – a Screamer – and she's transmitting this fear at viral speed to all the passengers around her.

Suddenly I know why I had misgivings about this trip. I'm writing the scene to come in my head: driven to distraction by our Screamer's frightened cries, and just as we actually take off – the moment of maximum danger – a passenger clicks out of his seat belt and throws himself at one of the doors, demanding to be let off the plane. A panicky fight ensues between the crazed passenger and the terrified stewardess, who's too small to... Stop. It's never going to happen. Or is it? As the plane leaves the ground with a roar of engine noise, the Screamer loses it completely. We turn round to see her unbuckling, and trying to wrestle out of her boyfriend's grip, yelling out at the top of her voice:

"We're all going to die!!!!!"

All the boyfriend can offer is a pathetic: "It'll all be alright, it'll be alright, it'll be alright."

I've had enough. With no sign of the attendants doing anything, and every sign that angry, nervous passengers are on the point of mutiny, I swivel round in my seat and hiss harshly through the gap between the seats:

"Harden the f up, will you!"

And despite Lou looking at me like I'm Cruella Deville, it kind of works.

*

The respite is short. As soon as we start to drop height for the descent, the Screamer starts to kick off again. By the time we get within 300 feet of the ground, she's wailing at full pitch while her companion pointlessly counts off the metres left to drop before we hit solid ground, but miraculously we bump down alive at Gatwick, in drizzle – of course – and watch resentfully along with the rest of the passengers as the Screamer is escorted off the plane ahead of everyone else by an airline first-aider and her totally wrung-out partner. Twenty minutes later, we've escaped the airport and set off in a hired car towards the festival site. It's not exactly cold, but it's hardly Mediterranean either, and the forecast isn't great. But as Lou drives us down deep, green Kentish lanes, I acknowledge that my new-found calm and contentment seems to be holding out better than expected. And there's another cause for hope: my intuition is that the hot flushes may actually be subsiding a bit, along with the anxiety, guilt and blood pressure levels. Maybe I'm imagining it; but maybe, just maybe, the rollercoaster is running out of gas.

We arrive at the field as the sky is going pale and easily find the rest of our mates, who have already set up camp, complete with a comfortable tent each, a private ladies' only chemical loo tent (bless Aggs) and a large, round, shared, 'sittingroom' tent with a big table, comfy seating, and plenty of food and wine supplies. Mike, O's father, who is the inspiration behind these annual gatherings, arrives in a crazy, vintage camper van rental. Mike is based in France now, but he's a conservation specialist who spends a lot of his time in inhospitable, often war-torn countries, so I don't get to see him very often. Mike's very committed to his work and very funny about its many fascinating challenges, so I can't wait to catch up on his latest adventures. The drizzle stops. The Grateful Dead tribute band arrives in a convoy of camper vans and immediately get out their equipment and start warming up on stage for a first night jam.

Slightly incongruously, they are all Parisian, all accomplished professional musicians who play with other bands or orchestras most of the year, and indulge themselves in revisiting psychedelic music just for the crack. But they're *really* good. And one of them, the bassist, instantly catches my eye. I'm not sure why. He looks cool and slightly mysterious, in a jazz-geek, specky, sixties kind of way. By the end of the jam session I've developed a kind of crush on him. Lou is amused by this and encourages me to go and talk to him, since artists and punters at the festival fraternise freely together (although mostly that means eating and drinking at the same hay-bale restaurant or using the same portaloos).

I'm too shy for that, and I've always been lousy at small talk, but I spend a very pleasant couple of hours, as the sun reappears to warm our backs before sunset and we settle down round the campfire with the first box of rosé, daydreaming a festival romance with specky-sexy-cool-bassist guy. I imagine myself wandering up to him in the beer tent, and impressing him with my colloquial French. I imagine sharing a drink or two... then he suggests a walk round the site... with the sun going down, we're standing under that massive oak tree looking back at the colourful, flag- strewn encampments ringing the stage, as he steps up very close, whispers some sexy French phrase that translates as 'I fancy the arse off you', and wraps me up in a long, sexy, jazz-geeky kiss...

Although the fantasy persists mildly over the next day, and despite further promptings from Lou, I'm still too much of a coward to even introduce myself to him and tell him I love the way he plays. What I do instead, over the course of the festival, is to stalk him, in a no-hassle, long-distance sort of way, as he mooches around the site in between sets or meals. I learn his routines: how many spliffs he shares with the band before breakfast, for example (two to three); how he likes his eggs (poché); even when he goes for a crap. I lurk in the shadow of the sound tent, or stare from behind the plastic curtains of our encampment sitting room as he pursues his seductively cool, laid-back schedule. Despite Lou's enthusiasm for a liaison – a bit of flirting would do me good, she says – I never get nearer to him than about ten yards.

Until the last night of the Party. I haven't had a shower since leaving France, and although Aggs's glam-camping facilities definitely exceed expectations, we've all had to make do with a wash in a basin of lukewarm water for the past two days, so I'm not looking or feeling or smelling my best. But none of that matters, because the rain has stopped, the evening is damp but warm, there's a funky blue-grass band playing and we're all down at the stage dancing ourselves stupid.

In fact, most of the campers are out of their tents and moving and grooving along in whatever way they feel appropriate; either that or they're standing around watching and sipping pints of fabulous micro-brewery ale supplied by the party organiser. Among the standers and watchers I suddenly spot cool-geeky-bassist guy only feet away from me. I'm sufficiently distracted by this to trip on a tussock as I dance and lurch towards him, knocking his pint of fabulous ale all over my hair and my remaining cleanish T-shirt. I apologise in French, then I offer to buy him a fresh beer (which he insists isn't necessary), and head off as quickly as I can to change my now beery top.

In my tent, I'm thinking about sexy bassist guy as I sort through my clothes by smell and put the least objectionable item back on. I decide I don't care that I've embarrassed myself in front of him. Right now, I don't really care too much about anything except getting back to the stage for more dancing. My hair smells of beer, though, so I pour a bit of last night's mineral water over my head, then towel off my hair, ready to return to the fray. As an afterthought I grab Lou's Tea Tree oil (she's been suffering from an itchy scalp) to spritz my hair with, then instantly regret the medicinal smell overlaying the hoppy perfume of the beer. No matter, I think. All I'm going to do is dance and get even more smelly. I step out of my tent and walk straight into cool-speccy-bassist guy.

"I see you come here," he says in charmingly awkward English. "I wait you."

"Right… cool…" I smile uncertainly. What's happening?

"You… speak French?" he asks sheepishly. "For me, English not so good."

He smiles apologetically. Warm, full, soft lips. Sexy.

"Pas de soucis, on parle Francais," I return, smiling back.

"Nickel, tu prends un verre avec moi au bar?"

OMG. He's asking me to have a drink with him. Before I've even begun to decide on my reaction I hear myself saying:

"Ouai, biensûr, si c'est moi qui paie." Sure, if I'm paying.

OMG, I said yes.

Ten minutes later, me and specky-sexy guy are installed on our very own, private hay bales, chewing the fat. He tells me about his life in Paris: he plays for a professional jazz band and his hobbies include making films about 'underground' culture and cooking. I tell him about writing for television, and how I ended up with a house in France, and how I ended up here. Except we're not *really* talking about stuff so much as eyeing each other up – playing that game I haven't played in sooooo long.

I wish I'd had a shower, avoided the tea-tree oil and done something with my hair now. And I wish it wasn't necessary to speak in another language, because I'm having trouble keeping up the cool French chat while engaging with my own internal convo about *what's going to happen next*. And what my response should be if it does. He's even nicer seen close up, and he comes across as mature and sane and funny, and I'm so flattered it's making me breathless, but the question is: am I going to do the right thing? What exactly is the right thing? I realise I've stopped talking and we're just watching each other.

"T'es mariée ou pas, toi?"

Here we go. He wants to know if I'm married.

"Non." It's the truth. Just not all the truth.

"Enorme." Great. He smiles another full-on, bedroom smile and leans suddenly towards me, his soft mouth opening. This is it.

He tastes nice. His sensitive, bass-playing hands slide up my torso from my waist as his kiss gets hotter. He grips my ribs, his thumbs sliding over the curve of my breasts, then pulls away gently:

"Trop de monde ici, non?" He nods round the bar. "On y va?"

OK. Now he's inviting me to go somewhere more private.

This really *is* it.

*

The live music has just finished and all my friends are back in the communal chill-out tent talking and drinking when I reappear. Aggs hands me a glass of rosé. Lou's straight in with the interrogation.

"So where have you been?" She leans towards me expectantly.

"Having a drink," I tell her with a smile.

"With him? Sexy bassist guy?"

"Yup."

"So did you score?"

"I had a very nice time," I reply evasively.

"C'mon. I need to know details."

"We kissed."

"Nice?"

"Yeah…"

"And…?"

"And then I told him I wasn't going back to his camper van."

"Why?" Lou sounds positively disappointed.

It's a question I was asking myself as soon as I'd walked away from openly disappointed sexy bassist guy at the bar. Did I say no because it would have been wrong to betray S, or because I was chicken, or because I didn't fancy him enough… or simply because, three days from my last shower, personal hygiene considerations asserted themselves? All of the above, I s'pose. To be perfectly honest though, what happened while I was being enfolded in sexy bassist guy's embrace is that I realized I didn't fancy him as much as the man I've been living with for the past twenty-something years. Strange… but true.

And anyway, by the time I left sexy bassist at the bar, I'd already got what I think I *really* wanted: a small but important piece of objective evidence that, despite all the ravages of the meno-rollercoaster, someone cool, French and maybe fifteen years younger than me thinks I'm attractive enough to pursue round a field in Kent, even when I smell. As I'm thinking this, I'm reminded how ruthlessly The Change has been gouging away my self-esteem – how differently I felt about myself just a few weeks before. I make a note to self: deploy all available strategies to fight getting back on the rollercoaster again. Except cheating on S, that is.

***

11. HIGH AND LOW (SEPTEMBER)

Summer's over. Boo. S has asked me to marry him. Hurrah! Kind of. I should be pleased about him deciding that now is the moment to legally cement our union, but there are 'ishoos'. One of them is that S's Mum has taken the glad tidings as an opportunity to have an extended moan: what do we mean, Register Office and no 'wedding breakfast'? What about the church service, the huge, unwieldy dresses, the massive, tiered cake with little him and her dolls on top, the stunningly expensive photographer to record the event, the truckload of costly, fast-wilting flowers, the confetti, the car done up with bows and foam and noisy streamers… and the hats???

There are so many negative answers to these questions that I'm at a loss where to start. I hate hats, for openers; I've never really enjoyed church weddings, number two; I'm so NOT photogenic that even S has trouble finding photos of me that he can convincingly claim he likes; I like cake, I guess – but that's not nearly a good enough reason to have an *OK!* Wedding; and I have never worn a really big dress or ever wanted to (if you exclude those crazy, full-length, frilly, Laura Ashley extravaganzas we all used to love when we were fourteen). Anyway, me and S have been happily 'living in sincerity' (as an old mate used to call it) for a quarter of a century.

S and I discuss the possibilities for compromise, but in the end what we decide is that it's our marriage, not anybody else's, so we take a deep breath and go over to explain this to Mum. The deep breath is literal not metaphorical, due to the fact that despite being in her 80s, Mum still chunders her way through sixty to eighty fags a day. (Luckily, she was well provided-for by S's late Dad, or she'd have to apply for hardship payments to keep up her cigarette run-rate.) She also feels the cold badly, so permission to open the window at her place requires an Act of Parliament. The result is that her large, three bed, two bath flat looks and smells like a military training ground after the smoke bombs go off, and a trip to the loo, unless you keep one hand on the wall at all times and draw yourself a mental map, or leave yourself a trail of breadcrumbs à la Hansel and Gretel, can be a one-way ticket to slow, panicky asphyxiation.

I risk sending S off to the kitchen in the hope that he'll make it back, preferably with a cup of tea. As he bravely disappears into the stale-smelling murk, I gently set out our thoughts and decisions, and invite Mum to come and celebrate with us on or around the day. None of our feelings or preferences cut much ice with Mrs. I'm-Officially-Disappointed, though. She declares our plan not to her liking and decides she won't be getting involved. Fine, I say – or rather I think this while maintaining an unwavering rictus smile – stay home then, and stew in the artificial champagne fountain of your imagination.

The other reason I'm not giddy with the happy peal of wedding bells is that S's motives for popping the matrimonial question are partly, at least, grimly practical. About a year ago my friend Belinda reminded us that if we're *not* married and some terrible accident befalls one of us, and that person needs emergency medical treatment or something like that, but is also unconscious or otherwise non-compos mentis, the other one doesn't have any right to decide what's best. In fact, he or she doesn't necessarily have the right to ring up and ask what's happening to the other one, unless we've got the bit of paper from the Register Office that says 'we are one'. We talked about getting married straight away, but put it off, mostly because wanting access to your loved one's deathbed is a bit of a miserable logline to a marriage announcement.

But getting home from France in a cheery, rejuvenated, sun-kissed frame of mind has brought out S's romantic streak. He's tried out referring to me as his wife a couple of times and apparently it's been a laugh. So we're doing it! We manage to get a booking quickly, because we're prepared to forego a Saturday lunchtime and turn up at nine o'clock on a Monday morning to tie the knot. My sister's going to be away on a jaunt to Paris with The Nipper (one her Dad's nicknames for Anna) so instead, Lou – our Maid of Dishonour – is going to come up and throw confetti at us or something similar, before she finally flies home to San Francisco. O and F have already agreed to be our witnesses, on condition that they have full rein to giggle, point and generally make fun of us for the day. No prob. I imagine we'll feel a bit stupid anyway.

We decide it's not a runner to have a party afterwards, because it'll be 9.30 on a Monday morning and therefore not an ideal moment for getting legless, so instead we agree on afternoon drinks the day before 'our big day'. That way we'll be able to share in the cheeriness with a few friends and family, get rid of everyone by evening, have a bit of food, a last glass of champagne and a reasonably early night, so as to be bright-eyed and bushy-tailed for marriage in the morning. That's the theory.

Sunday dawns warm and sunny. Lou arrives off the London train in party mood. S and I fridge a load of champagne. F arrives with a secret wedding cake (baking is one of the things she excels at) and O arrives with all the necessaries for a proper cocktail bar (cocktails is one of the things he excels at). Then a chef friend who's offered to do the nibbles appears with a car full of delicious looking raw materials that he's planning to cook up into 'proper' finger food. All good. We put a couple of tables and some extra chairs in the garden and relax to await the arrival of our guests.

Six or seven hours later, the house is brimming with drink and people and there's little sign of anything slowing down. O's cocktails have put everyone in an excessively good mood, the food ditto, and to my big surprise, I'm feeling genuinely excited about becoming Mrs S in a matter of hours. And I'm not the only one. Lou, who's imbibed enough champagne and cocktails to fill my roll top bath, has a particularly bright glint in her eye as she drags me into her bedroom for a quick word. I wonder if she's planning to give me wedding night advice, but that's not at all what she's got in mind…

"You know that Blondie with the pony tail?" she says in a slightly slurred, conspiratorial whisper.

"You mean O's mate?"

"Yeah. He's fit, don't you think?"

Uh-oh. "I guess. What's your point?"

"My point is… I think I'm gonna take him back to his place and shag him."

Lou says this with a wicked, cat-about-to-get-cream-type grin.

I'm gobsmacked. "What? Now?"

She nods. "He's made *his* feelings clear. And it's been years since I was in this sort of mood."

She's actually serious…

"So as long as you're sure he's not an axe-murderer or a pervert..."

"No way, he's a really safe guy…" I defend him instinctively.

Except suddenly I'm thinking that was the wrong answer. She's 57. Blondie is 29 – plus, in my mind, he'll always be a shy teenager with a proto-tash, a sweet (and almost certainly heavily-drugged) smile and feet far too big for the rest of him. To complicate things further, Lou is not that long ago separated from Julia, her partner of fifteen years, and is also, I can't help calling to mind, stepmum to Julia's two twenty-something lads. Is shagging a kid her stepsons' age who she barely knows really gonna work out for her?

"So what do you think?" Another grin.

It's now or never. Either I lie and tell her he's a BNP activist and homophobe, with horrific breath and a really unpleasant, communicable disease that's not obvious until you get his boxers off… or…

"What the hell – if you're both up for it… go for it."

Lou grins the wicked grin again. "D'you reckon this makes me a cougar, then?"

"Yeah, I'm not sure… to be honest, I think we've already crossed cougar territory, babe… we're now plodding breathlessly up into the high ground where the snow leopards hang out."

Lou is undaunted. "Whatever. I'll only be a couple of hours. Keep some champagne on ice for my return."

And with that she's off. I say nothing to O or S as I watch the happy couple grab their jackets and a quick slobbery kiss on the doorstep, before they jog off down the path, hand in hand, laughing and happily hungry for each other. You've gotta hand it to her, I think. That's one way to fight the signs of ageing…

*

Two and a half hours later, Lou slips back into the party with a reassuringly satisfied look on her face.

"I did it!" she announces to me with a punch of the air as she helps herself to a fresh glass of fizz in the kitchen.

"But did you have a *good time* doing it?"

"Yeah!"

"Both of you?"

"Best night he's ever had – shame he probably won't remember it!" She cracks another wicked grin. "Wham bam, thank you ma'am."

I laugh and forgive her the Americanism. I'm proud of her for not being a past-it, unadventurous, old 50-something. I'm proud of her for having the courage and the desire to ignore all the good reasons *not* to take Blondie off and shag him. And I'm really proud of her for actually managing to enjoy herself and show him a good time too.

"You're the hottest snow leopard in town," I tell her as I hug her hard.

She grins back. "You bet... only... don't say anything to anyone else for now, okay?"

"Kay. Why not?"

"There's a tiny complication," she says, looking suddenly sheepish.

My mind goes into instant overdrive on what that complication might be: pregnancy??? Not possible. A new girlfriend she hadn't told me about? Equally unlikely. STD? It seems improbable that Blondie, who's a nice boy, would have said yes if he was in danger of giving Lou anything more lasting than a fun couple of hours...

"I need you to call Blondie for me. "

"Really? Why?"

"Cause... well, when we got over to his place, I decided that keeping my hearing aids in might be a bit of a passion-killer..."

"You're not wrong, hon," I nod, as the image starts to make me chuckle.

"... so I discreetly took them out before we, y'know..."

"Good thinking, so...?"

"Problem is... I thought I'd put them in my pocket, but now I can't find them anywhere. I'm thinking I must've left them there... *in his bedroom.*"

Our eyes lock as the thought sinks in. She, the hot but hard-of-hearing snow leopard, looks back at me with comically raised eyebrows. I can see her problem. She's disinclined to blow her lover cover by calling up to ask for her hearing aids back. I can feel laughter bubbling up.

"Can't you... wouldn't it be less embarrassing to just... view it as a collateral loss and get some more hearing aids?"

Lou shrugs. "I would... but they cost more than 500 dollars a pop..."

"Jeez," I say, half to myself. "Guess I'd better make the call then." But Lou hasn't heard me.

"Say again?

"I was just thinking..."

"You what...?"

I crack up. Lou cracks up. And once we've started we can't stop. We laugh so hard that we have to hide in the utility room for ten minutes, and when we reappear, S thinks we're having some kind of strange, female, pre-nuptial crying crisis.

The last invitee leaves at five that morning. Less than five hours later, me, S, Lou, O and F are walking down the road back from the Register Office, all of us still drunk, with S waving our marriage certificate at the traffic like Loadsamoney with his wad, and our entourage blowing bubbles and throwing confetti in our path. I'm feeling very tired, a bit sick and having a massive, probably alcohol-induced, hot flush. But I couldn't be happier.

*

Everything is cyclical. Sure. You wouldn't know what happiness was if you hadn't experienced the opposite. I guess. No one gets to be happy all the time. Why not? So I'm still in the post-nuptial bliss phase, or at least I'm still getting a kick out of the novelty of being a wife, when I wake up one morning with an aching pain in my upper chest. It's not all that bad, and it's limited to one particular spot, a couple of inches under my left clavicle. I am amazingly calm, given my condition. It's probably not the heart attack, I reassure S, but it definitely warrants a trip to the surgery and, it turns out a couple of hours later, an appointment at the walk-in xray department at the Norfolk and Norwich University Hospital on the edge of town. Modern technology being what it is, the pictures of my chest are available electronically to the perky young Australian radiologist doing the xray almost immediately, on his computer.

"There's definitely something there," the radiologist says as he stares at his screen.

"What sort of something?"

"Hard to tell that from an x-ray. What I *can* tell you is that whatever it is, it measures about three by three centimetres, and I reckon the doc'll order up a CT scan ASAP."

"Okay..." I can feel fear coursing up from my stomach and wrapping round my chest. "Can you give me an idea... of the possibilities?".

"Not my aisle, I'm afraid," he answers chirpily. "They'll get you in for the scan as soon as they can, then a consultant will be able to give you the full lowdown."

"How long will I have to wait for the scan?"

"Waiting lists are fairly short at the mo – prob'ly about four to five weeks."

"Five weeks!" I say to S, as I accept the reassuring cup of tea he offers me on my return. "I can't believe we've got to wait that long to even know what's going on..."

"It's probably nothing," S says semi-convincingly. "You've been really healthy recently... and you look great!"

"I guess. But I've been noticing I get a bit breathless after I run up the stairs."

Until I say it, I hadn't even thought about this, but now I realise that it's been going on for a while and I'd put it down to relapse smoking and drinking too much on holiday.

"I get breathless running upstairs too," S counters.

"Sure you do – if you're climbing the Eiffel Tower. I'm talking about making it from the kitchen to the front door."

S frowns. "So what do you want to do?"

"I just want to know. Now."

I've always hated the fact that if you can pay, and only if you can pay, you simply jump the queue and get specialist medical help as soon as you need it. I feel the same massive resentment about inequality of education. It's a crime against our common future. But I'm a coward too. Faced with weeks of waiting and not knowing, worrying and imagining, my first instinct is to get out my cheque book. I get the name of a consultant who does private appointments. I call his secretary. A week later, I've had a scan and S and I are sitting in a quiet, comfortable waiting room with tea and coffee on tap, being apologized to by a very nice nurse about having to wait five minutes to see the Consultant. Shortly thereafter, we're called into the private consulting room of a friendly man in his 30s in a crisp blue shirt.

After brief pleasantries, the Consultant says he's going to show us what the scan has picked up. He clicks something on his computer and a series of strange, pulsating, multi-coloured images of The Thing In My Chest appear, which are very hard for us to interpret. He asks me a bunch of alarmingly obvious questions: do I have a cough; have I felt unwell; am I losing weight; how much did I used to smoke and for how long... I answer politely, but in my head I'm begging him to stop asking and start answering.

"Can you tell me what you think it is?" I finally ask, as calmly as possible.

"There are two possibilities." The Consultant turns away from his computer and looks at me steadily.

"Either you have had a chest infection without knowing it, something like pneumonia, and this has caused some damage... or, the growth is some sort of tumour."

"Meaning it's lung cancer."

"Yes. Although in a very small number of cases, a tumour can be benign."

Then I have to ask... although I don't really want the answer to this: "Can you say which of the alternatives you think is the most likely?"

The Consultant looks back at the screen and the pulsing technicolour images of The Thing. He turns back to me and frowns. His voice is kind but firm.

"Considering the number of years you've been a smoker... I think I'd have to say there's at least a sixty percent chance that it's cancerous."

Back home, S and I are quiet. Numb. We hug for a while. S makes us a nice, reassuring cup of tea. We sit and review the situation. The medical strategy, as explained by the Consultant, is that I take a large quantity of two different antibiotics for three weeks, then I have another scan and another appointment with the Consultant. If The Thing has shrunk, that means it's almost certainly an infection. If it hasn't, it's more 'investigations', possibly biopsies, and then a diagnosis and a plan for treatment, if indeed it's not too late for all that. We're in limbo for a month.

A hot flush floods through me. Strangely, it doesn't make me feel irritated or self-pitying. In fact, quite the opposite. I experience an unexpected surge of nostalgia: good old hot flushes... Now that I'm in Disaster's waiting room, being menopausal feels like a positive assertion of Life. So what if it signals a loss of genitourinary tension? At least it's just a phase, rather than an end to everything.

Maybe now I'll never get to the end of this phase. Lung cancer's got a very bad rep for killing people quickly, as I know from my own internet abuse. Will I die before my hair goes grey, or my hearing gives out or my bones go brittle, or I get to be a Grandma? Will I die before my sister (a question I've particularly avoided confronting all my life, because either answer provokes immediate despair)? And if I do die, will I be brave about it? And will all the people I love be okay without me? I don't know. All I know is that I've got to wait forty-four thousand, six hundred and forty more minutes on hold.

***

12. STAYING ALIVE (OCTOBER)

I'm on a deadline for the script-doctoring job I got just before we left France – probably a good thing in the circumstances. I like the main character and the plot, which had serious problems but was starting to come together quite nicely before all this happened. But now work's a struggle: fiction feels kind of pointless in the face of today's hard fact. And after all the months of obsessing about it one way or another, I'm now at a loss *what* to think about the possibility that *I might actually be dying*. There's an odd sense of relief on one level: at least I know which of the huge cast of worst-case-scenarios I'm going to be dealing with. I keep thinking about Spike Milligan's epitaph: "I told you I was ill".

I haven't told the people I'm working for, though, for now. Apart from anything else, if I *am* dying, we'll need all the cash we can get our hands on. And although I know they'd be sympathetic, the raw truth is that the production company I've been commissioned by needs the product to sell, and if I can't deliver because I'm having chemo or something, they'll look for someone else who can.

When my Dad died – he was a writer too – I phoned his publisher because he'd just finished a first draft of his latest novel. I asked the Publisher straight up what kind of advance, if any, he might be offering for the novel, and suggested that, since writing was my business too, I could possibly take over the reins and make any changes to the manuscript that were required before publication.

The Publisher was very nice. So nice that I couldn't unravel what he was actually telling me to start with. When the penny dropped, the headline was that since my Dad was dead, he probably wouldn't be writing another five books in the series. Ergo, the publishers' investment suddenly lacked future prospects. Ergo, he was terribly sorry, but they weren't any longer interested. That's just the way it works.

After he died, my Dad got an obituary in *The Guardian* because he'd written loads of 'cult' television through the sixties and seventies. It tracks pretty routinely through his many writing credits and suggests, quite rightly, that his TV work was bigger on quantity than quality, and a lot of his novels were 'airport reads', whereas he deserved the critical acclaim he got for his two memoirs, *Worlds End* and *White City*. The obit ends with a brief summary of his personal history:

> *'His memoirs garnered welcome if belated critical acclaim. His first and third wives predeceased him, and his second marriage ended in divorce; he is survived by the twin daughters of his first marriage.'*

The rest of the piece, I wasn't bothered by, either way. But the bleak (and factually incorrect) closing image of the oft-divorced, under-acclaimed, probably lonely writer conjured up in that last line annoyed me quite a lot at the time. I didn't mind what people thought about my Dad's *writing*. But I did want posterity to have an accurate picture of *who* he was.

In fact, up to the day he dropped dead suddenly, with a glass of wine in his hand while he chatted with my sister, my Dad believed that he was one of the luckiest people on earth. He was a man people didn't forget – popular, wise, warm, strong, clever and full of empathy. He was happy spending a lot of time alone with his work, but he was also kind, sensitive, always interested and always moved by peoples' triumphs and tragedies. People admired my Dad. As teenagers, a whole bunch of our friends had crushes on him. He'd been married three times and was in a strong, fourth relationship when he died, but he'd never lost the love, respect or friendship of his former wives, or their families and friends. I would have liked the obit to reflect the simple fact that his life was rich, fulfilling, and deservedly full of the rewards of being one of the good guys.

What will posterity think of me, if anything? I won't be getting an obituary anywhere, that's for sure. I was once the subject of an article in *The Guardian* by Nancy Banks Smith, because I'd written episodes for two 'flagship' crime drama series that were transmitted simultaneously on ITV and BBC one night. The title of the article was 'Woman of Mystery', although I managed to ruin any impact this might have had by offering banal, demystifying answers to all Nancy's questions when she called out of the blue to talk to me (I was on a massive deadline at the time). So what is my legacy? A stack of TV dramas, a couple of history books and a few blogs? I like to think that I've stayed true to my folks' values, and that my bit of the family extension retains the loving, positive approach to life that my parents and grandparents were so good at. But is that anywhere near enough? Have I *done living justice*?

*

A week into the Big Wait, I'm in a very strange space, tense and trance-like, as if I'm being drip-fed something psychotropic with added hypochondria. I'm outside of myself, and everything else, looking in. I try to distract myself but I can't stop self-examining every two minutes, and deciding that I've got a new pain or a disturbing 'funny feeling'. Belinda, who's a veteran of various personal health dramas, says that this is entirely normal and most likely stress-induced and I'm sure she's right, but having a rational explanation isn't helping reduce these scary little episodes one bit.

I'm desperate to get the month over with and know whether I'll ever be seeing France or considering a change of dishwasher tablet brands again. But on the other hand, I don't want to waste or wish away a single second of time if it can be avoided. Suddenly, Time is precious, and so is pretty much everything else. Staring at the world from the perspective of The End has turned me overnight into a hopeless romantic. I literally ache with the beauty of the dawn and the silvery, shimmery quality of the light in East Anglia. I'm affected beyond reason by the Town Hall clock, striking the hours out over the city. I can't get enough of the colour of beetroot or the feel and smell of S's skin. But there are some things that have completely lost their attraction: sunset and bedtime are both pretty crap; reading is too hard to focus on; watching TV is out because cancer pops up one way or another every few minutes; spending time with family is precious but poignant – and all discussion of the next World Cup (from which I may well be absent) is just too depressing.

I force myself to go shopping, and pass my favourite Big Issue seller as usual. Now, my problem isn't that I envy him his fags. Instead I'm utterly gobsmacked that although he only eats proper food once a month and stands out in the wind and rain all day looking like Ozzie Osbourne in a shipwreck, he's managing to hold onto the gift of Life, whereas I've quite possibly just left mine on the bus. How did that happen? And it's not just the Big Issue seller. I wander round the market, noticing for the first time how many people appear to be too sick, mad, ancient or morbidly obese to keep breathing for a single second longer, but are carrying on anyway.

Nothing's making much sense. I've noticed a paradigm shift in my attitude to domestic chores – ironing, buying loo cleaner and tidying up: now, the question is why? I make myself do a bit, but what *is* the point in keeping my drawers tidy or making stock for the freezer? I don't know the answer. From there, it's only a short step to asking why I do anything. Why am I alive? What do I live *for*? I live because living is great, I say to myself. And I live to enjoy sharing stuff with other people, obviously, and to contribute where I can. But if everyone I knew and/or loved suddenly disappeared, what would be my existential justification? Would there be one? Life has always been *everything*, the only thing. Now it feels like a fragile sideshow to *not* being, to Nothing.

I've lost all interest in cooking, so we're back to a costly going-out-for-dinner regime. My appetite's fast disappearing in any case. Even S, normally a big eater, is having trouble getting enough calories down him. I've managed to get a draft of my script re-write off to the producers, but I'm officially down with 'a bad chest infection' now, and I've warned them that I won't be available for further work for a week or two. In fact, I'm feeling so utterly becalmed by the necessity to Wait And See that replacing a toilet roll feels like an achievement.

We should be updating our wills, but I can't bring myself to commit anything to paper, just in case I make it come true. Most of my 'estate' will simply pass on to S anyway, but as I prowl round the house, staring wanly at particular items and objects that I might want to gift to individuals, I feel like I'm evaporating. All that will soon remain of me, quite possibly, is contained within the four walls of this house: my books, my teapot collection, my Tesco clubcard points and a fine portrait of my maternal great grandmother. Who and what I am is seeping away.

I decide to try swimming again. On a positive level, I tell S, it's a way of thinking myself well. Or, more pessimistically – I keep this to myself – it's a way of continually assessing my deterioration. If I've got lung cancer, I'll be able to measure my reducing life expectancy in 50-metre lengths. I've got a similar assessment system in mind around eating cake. I don't even like cake much, but I've decided to eat loads of it and see what happens to my weight. If I keep losing it, that will tell me something. It's a scary thought. But I can't help wanting to *know.*

My first time back at the UEA pool, I make S come with me, just in case I have a panic attack or expire in mid-stroke. I'm outside myself again, watching as I get changed into my swimming costume and chat to a nice lady in her seventies who swims every day. She asks me how I am and compliments me on having 'kept my figure'. I don't tell her that the reason for that might be that there's something monstrous eating away at me from inside. I'm fine, I tell her. How are you? But I don't listen to the answer.

In the pool, I'm so focused on my breathing or lack of it, that I nearly drown after four lengths. I suggest self-pityingly to S that I should just give up. He tells me it's all psychological. He points out that I was perfectly capable of swimming a matter of days ago. Nothing can have changed that quickly. I fight this simple logic, but he's probably right. Possibly. But I can also feel The Thing, I tell him. It doesn't exactly hurt, but now that I know it's there, and it's a lump, and it has a certain size, I can't help feeling it, heavy in my upper chest. In my mind it's really ugly too: a misshapen bloody mass of stuff with blobby lumps of tissue and veins and... S tells me to stop. The description is making him queasy.

We set off again, S doing his neat, elegant crawl in the lane next to me, and leaving me quickly behind, while I slow down and try and match my pace to my available lung power. I feel The Thing as I stretch my arms out and round for each stroke. I wonder how long it's been there. I meander mentally back through the months, looking for the point at which I noticed I was puffing up the stairs, but it's elusive. Wait a minute, though... Did it start after I had that couple of days in bed in January? I had a temperature *and a cough*. I'd forgotten about that. I experience a small but powerful physical frisson – a hopeful surge of adrenalin that transmits itself to my arms and legs. Maybe it *is* an infection. Maybe I've had this lump for months and months without realizing it. Maybe I'm not dying after all. And even if the Thing is cancerous, I suddenly decide, I'm not going to give up on myself. Not *everyone* dies of lung cancer.

I push harder and faster through the water, bringing my own physical strength to bear and focusing all my thoughts on the Thing, willing it to get smaller. Perhaps if I concentrate *all* my powers on it, I can stop it in its tracks. In fact, I'm suddenly determined. I will overcome it. I will think and swim it away. Head down, I increase my pace and power back and forth, oblivious to everything but my new mission. It's a bit giddy-making, like being drunk, but in a positive, empowered sort of way. I'm so locked into extirpating my cancer through power breast-stroke that I haven't noticed that the whole of the pool has just emptied in preparation for the lowering of its floor (this happens every day just before the swim and exercise classes begin). While I've been busy beating The Thing into submission, S has been waving and calling out (he later explains), trying to get my attention while about thirty other pool users have been sitting on the side watching and waiting.

I get to one end and feel a firm hand grip my shoulder. Startled, I stop and look up through my heavily tinted goggles. I see a young pool guard leaning over me, and my cozzy-clad audience staring back at me with quizzical and annoyed expressions.

"Sorry, but you've got to stop and get out," he says. "Just for a minute".

I want to tell him – everyone – that that's impossible. I'm engaged in an elemental struggle. I'm fighting for my life. I'm *on it.* Aquafit will just have to wait. But all I actually say is: "Sure. Sorry."

*

17 October. It's my birthday. Our more accurately it's *our* birthday. I get on the scales to see if I've put on any cake-weight. I haven't lost any more, but I haven't gained any either. Shit.

Normally I love this day. I'm not bothered about presents or parties or doing anything in particular. I just enjoy the fact that since it's 'our special day', I can indulge myself however I want, if I want. Often, I just end up calling Caroline for a chat, then working on as usual. Or I might buy myself a super-expensive bunch of amazing flowers, or do nothing but drink champagne and read a book all evening. Our birthday also tends to be a moment for looking forward. Normally there's a future to imagine: an unsignposted but exciting territory of possibilities. But now there's none of that. The Future's on a warning. There's just The Present, most of which is horrible, and The Past.

And there's blood. I'm not sure what significance, if any, to attach to the fact that I've started bleeding on my birthday, but right now, as with the hot flushes, having a period feels like evidence of a sort that my body isn't giving up on everything quite yet. S brings me coffee and the papers in bed for entertainment while the painkillers kick in. I scan the news, but in line with my current mortality mindset, I'm avoiding issues of the moment, and thinking about the past, and the very first time I woke up bleeding.

I was eleven, and sharing a large, lofty room in our apartment in Cambridge, Massachusetts, with my sister, when I sat up in bed to discover that my pyjama bottoms were covered in blood. Although my Mum had talked us through the upcoming business of menstruating, and because I'd never seen anyone *really* bleeding, I'd imagined that the blood loss would be equivalent to having a cut finger at worst, so I was more than a bit alarmed to wake up soaked in the stuff. By contrast, my Mum was incredibly excited and tearful and gave me a day off school, took me out to lunch to celebrate being a *real woman* and bought me a gold-plated necklace that I kept for years and years. I remember while we were having our celebration lunch, my Mum describing what had been expelled by my body as 'an egg', which I found confusing, because it didn't anywhere near cover the brief but bloody experience I'd had.

It was the following summer – during which time I'd had a few proto-periods – that I'd ended up on the Costa del Sol with blond Brad The Beautiful. We'd met at the pool of the apartment complex where both our families were staying, and my Dad had invited his family to join us at a paella restaurant that evening. While the grown-ups were chatting and swapping info about the resort, and Caroline was keeping Brad's older sister busy, me and Brad had spent the evening stealing looks at each other and trying to think of things to talk about.

I remember how amazed and grateful I was that beautiful Brad was prepared to signal his interest in me so unequivocally. Up until then, the whole business of reading the runes of male attraction had remained a total mystery, even more mysterious than why we were made to wear *two* pairs of knickers at school (one normal, the other huge and baggy and made of dark blue material so rough it chafed your legs all the time). Tonight, though, I was wearing my own choice of knickers, and I was pretty sure that if I could arrange it right, I was on for The Kiss.

After supper, down on the beach (I'd been granted half an hour before my Dad came looking), we walked and talked, but I wasn't really concentrating on where he went to high school, or what his family was doing in Europe, because I was entirely focused on the moment, possibly only seconds away now, when he would bend over me from his impossible height, and the earth would tilt on its axis as his full, sweet-as-apple-pie lips parted, and his tongue found mine. I'd seen this so many times on TV that I was fairly confident I knew what it would feel like and what to do in response.

But The Kiss, when it came, didn't stick to the script. It was way better than that. At the time I thought it was the most incredible thing that had ever happened to me. The earth didn't move so much as my whole body ignited in voracious flames of lust. Brad seemed to quite like it too. As the palm trees waved, and the sea lapped, and the moonlight caught the angles of our young brown bodies entwined, I suddenly thought I knew what ecstasy felt like.

I couldn't sleep all night for replaying those few gloriously over-excited minutes on the beach at the mercy of my libido, and anticipating more of the same in the days to come. I was sure that this was love and I was in it. It was more than a bummer, therefore, when I skipped out of our apartment early the next morning to head for the pool and my assignation with Brad, to discover from his mum that he'd been taken seriously ill with food poisoning and was spewing his guts out into the toilet bowl of his en suite bathroom. Half an hour later, the arrival of my first *real* period confined me to my bed for more or less the rest of our stay. Poor me... and oh yeah, poor Brad.

Trying to manage periods in the days before technology was brought to bear on the design of sanitary equipment was frankly mucky. Back in the 70s, sanitary towels were no more sophisticated than a two-inch, thick wedge of wadding that you were supposed to keep in place by attaching it front and back to a belt worn under your knickers. Problem was, it didn't work. As soon as you moved, it would start to slip forward or back. A couple of hours in, however snug your knickers were, the wad was so heavy and sticky with blood that it felt like you had an oversized sirloin steak slung loosely between your legs (or creeping up your backside). It made even *walking* difficult, let alone things like playing sport.

I remember my total triumph the first time I managed to insert a tampax up my vagina – probably about a year after Brad, the beach and first blood. I took so long fiddling about and pushing the thing around that I managed to make myself really sore, but as soon as I'd got the damn thing rammed far enough up that it didn't fall out again moments later, I strolled out of our flat like a medal winner, glorying in the certainty that I'd never have to keep a steak in my knickers again, and feeling like a proper grown-up woman, despite the fact that I was in school uniform and heading for a double Latin lesson.

I've been thinking a lot about firsts and lasts: the first time I had grown-up sex in a bed (Turnham Green, 1969); the last time I spent an afternoon with my beloved Nana before she had her stroke (Putney, 1999). I've been rootling through old photo albums, picking out people and moments: my Dad looking dark-eyed and griefstricken just after my

Grandad died and just before me and Caroline were leaving to live in the States; me and Caroline and my Mum after my second stepdad died, trying to be cheerful on a holiday in Spain...

I've also been missing my Mum and my Nana, *really* missing them, for the first times in ages. I realise this is all part of getting older, this hold that the past and memory and loss begins to have over people. And the fact that my death is now a proximate possibility rather than a distant impossibility is adding to the tendency. But I'm fine with sticking with the past today. I'm perfectly aware that it's an escapist bolthole, but for now meandering around my back pages with my nearest and dearest (alive and dead) offers some relief from the maddening pause button on everything else.

*

Seven hundred and forty-four hours, eighteen restaurant dinners, thirty miserable nights and one CT scan later, the Wait is done, and me and S are back at the private hospital for the consultation. We're both in a state of advanced, suppressed panic. Other patients are sitting around in the lobby as we arrive, waiting to see other consultants. I overhear discussions about sports injuries and kidney infections and envy them their non-life-threatening problems. I'm so nervous that I think I'm going to be sick all over the Consultant's shiny shoes as he arrives to shake hands and escort us into his office, his face unreadable as before. He sits us down next to him, then turns to his screen.

"You remember the pictures from your first scan?" he says. S and I look at each other. Is he prevaricating? Holding back the bad news?

"Here's what we could see the first time."

He clicks onto the pulsating series of multi-coloured images I remembered from before.

"And now this is the latest..."

He clicks onto a second series. I look at S again. It's clear from his expression that they look more or less the same to him, as they do to me. This is bad news. I can't stand it anymore.

"Is it bigger or smaller?" I ask straight out.

"It was about three centimeters before. Now it's about half that size," the Consultant says evenly.

We struggle to take this in. "So that's good news?" S manages to ask.

"Yes," says the Consultant. "I'll want to see you again in six months, just to see how you're getting on, but I think I can say that the lump is now resolving, consistent with you having had a pneumonia-like infection."

Outside, having shaken hands again, and floated back through the patients waiting in the lobby of the hospital, for whom I'm suddenly feeling unending sympathy, S and I walk away, hand in hand, in floods of happy tears. En route back to the car, we keep stopping every few seconds, looking for confirmation from each other that we're not imagining this, and that I really am okay. We can't take it in. Life had galloped off and hidden somewhere, but now it's back. The Future's back too. And everyday concerns. Luxury.

***

13. AFTERLIFE (NOVEMBER)

As part of the 'I'm not dying after all' celebrations, Caroline and I have arranged a weekend get together in the North Norfolk countryside with our whole gang of old school friends. In line with what have come to be known as 'extreme reunions' (occasional weekends when we ditch the families and spend time together, reverting to old habits), I suggest a holiday cottage somewhere on the coast near me. I'm anticipating a couple of days of cooking, eating, drinking, walking to the pub, playing rounders on the beach and thoroughly unpacking the menopause and the business of ageing with my best girl mates.

"Sounds unmissable," says S, without quite managing to sound sincere.

They're all younger than me and Caroline, and therefore unlikely to be sharing my pain exactly, but at least I can count on them being interested and sympathetic. I get on the internet and find a cottage on the coast that looks perfect. It's going to cost a thousand pounds for the weekend, but it's large enough to accommodate all twelve of us (in shared double beds), it's round the corner from the George and Dragon, a walk to the sea, it looks cosy and comfortable in the pics, and it's described as a 'unique artist's home' in 'shabby chic, laid back' style, which suits us perfectly. The plan is that everyone will arrive at my house for a cuppa on Friday afternoon, then we'll drive out to the coast together in as few cars as are necessary.

It's shitty weather as the first carload arrives, but the rain is hardly dampening spirits. S makes tea while the gals sit around chatting and checking off what they've brought to take with us – essentially enough food and drink to maintain a Special Forces unit for several weeks. An hour later, we've squeezed ourselves, our supplies, our bags, and the biggest leg of lamb anyone's ever seen (brought by Sue from her very own Scottish farm) into three cars, and we're driving into Cley in the slightly murky dusk. We're due to meet the cottage owner, Mrs. K, at her home, collect the keys, hand over the dosh, get directions to the cottage and begin our weekend. That's the plan.

The address is easy to find. We pull up outside a pretty, flat-fronted terrace of large, flint-faced cottages set back from the road, just off the main village street. Caroline and I jump out to go and collect the keys. We knock on the door. A late middle-aged woman answers it. She's big, full-cheeked and pink, with a lot of dyed blonde hair scooped up on top of her head; and she's eccentrically dressed in many layers of rustic, floral print garments, giving the slight impression of a giant, over-upholstered folk costume doll. Creepy. She also appears to be in something of a hurry. But this is North Norfolk, so I'm reasonably chilled about it.

Mrs. K beckons us briskly into the cottage. As we comply, I notice that it looks pretty skuzzy. Her hallway is in a poor condition, paint peeling and covered in cobwebs. There seems to be plaster coming off the walls in lumps, and I can see some very strange wiring to what looks like a pre-world-war-two table lamp, sitting next to a pre-world-war-two telephone. The main room we've entered is a riot of ancient, dusty furniture and accessories, as if her home doubles as a bric-a-brac shop. Not a good advertisement... but hey, don't worry about it, I tell myself. It's not our problem.

Mrs. K is now explaining to Caroline that, contrary to the information given in the listing for the cottage, there is no internet connection, and the mobile signal out here is fairly hit and miss, but there's an internet café in Blakeney a few miles down the road if we need one. A spike of irritation pushes through my good mood. She also tells us that because she lives in the cottage herself some of the time, there are two rooms full of her possessions that are off limits. Well, okay... although I'm wondering why she needs to live in two places in the same village. But Caroline's telling her that's fine with us. Mrs. K asks for the cash and we hand it over. Mrs. K heads for the front door. We follow.

"I'm sorry," I say, "but you haven't told us how we find the cottage..."

Mrs. K stops with her hand on the door latch.

"This *is* the cottage," she answers slightly querulously. "And a precious home, that I hope you'll care for as well as enjoy." Before we can think of any reasonable response to this, she's out and off at a brisk walk down the path. Caroline and I stare at each other for a moment.

"Did she really say...?"

"Yeah..."

I step out onto the path, but Mrs. K is no longer to be seen. She's disappeared, despite her highly-coloured bulk, into the North Norfolk mist.

I step back inside. "She's gone!"

"Don't worry about it, hon," Caroline soothes.

"But this *can't* be *it*."

"I think you'll find it is." says Caroline, as she dumps her handbag on the table and looks round the room.

"It's a total dump!"

"Not arguing there," Caroline concedes evenly.

I turn back to the door. "I've really got to get her back here..."

Caroline stops me: "Hold on, we've barely seen round it yet. "

"This is bad enough!" I scan the room again. "It looks like Robin Williams' den in *Fisher King*."

"Don't exaggerate. Let's go get the girls."

We release the women from the cars, while I explain that we've just been conned by a creepy, giant folk doll of a native, and Caroline suggests we suck it up and go and explore the cottage before we unpack our stuff. As we gather in the hallway, I'm tense and apologizing. But the gals are firmly on a holiday high and full of the familiar excitement of being together for a session. Deciding to choose bedrooms first, they swarm up the stairs and start opening doors.

I'm still moaning as Caroline and I follow them, pick a door and enter a room that smells of damp. It looks dingy and uncared for. There are dead moths all over the carpet and yellowed newspaper sellotaped over the fanlight above the door. The third thing I notice is an unwrapped, half eaten Kit Kat on one of the bedside tables. Is this a joke? As I pull open the top drawer of a bow-fronted chest, causing the mirror propped up on it to slip down the back, it's full of stuff. So are all the other drawers. Caroline opens the cupboard. It's full of clothes too. Now I'm really irritated. We've stumbled into some kind of mad hoarder's house, she's fleeced us for a grand, and we haven't even been left anywhere to hang up our stuff! Caroline dismisses this as unimportant. We're only here for the weekend after all. We can store everything in our bags. You bet, I say. I'm not getting any of my clothes out anyway, in case of contamination…

A sudden shriek issues from the bedroom next door. Jayne is tending to Susie, who has a cut and bleeding finger. We wrap it in tissues while she explains that they were both at the window, trying to open it to let out the damp air, when they noticed a piece of cutlery – an old bone handled knife – had been wedged between the top and bottom sashes. Susie was trying to pull open the bottom sash as Jayne, without thinking, removed the knife. Susie just managed to react as the upper sash guillotined downwards, catching her finger instead of her whole hand.

Now I'm angry. You can't rent a cottage to people with that sort of safety issue unresolved. I'm determined to confront Mrs. K immediately, but not only has she disappeared... when I think about it, I've got no idea how to contact her in an emergency. We've only communicated by email, so I don't have a mobile number to call. I experience another flood of irritation and self-loathing. The girls calm me down. It'll be fine, they say.

Another shriek of laughter. We muster in what Lilly and SJ have just named the Asylum Seekers' room, since it consists of a metal bed, a broken sink with a rusty cold tap, and one bare-bulbed light, ideal for interrogation purposes only. Yet another cackle takes us to the bathroom. It's a large, cluttered, dusty but functional room with an old iron bath, an avocado basin and loo, and a pine built in cupboard containing plenty of (old) sheets and towels. But… the light pull controlling the ceiling light has just come off in Anna's hand, so it looks like it'll be on all weekend. And Anna also points out a metal, retro-deco wall light over the sink, which is hanging off the wall, suspended only by its own, fully- exposed wiring… Jeez! The place is lethal!

I issue firm instructions to all that nobody should use the sink or go near the wall light as we head back downstairs, but not before we've opened the last door onto a cobwebby room housing a substantial menagerie of huge, evil-smelling stuffed geese with angry eyes, and a large, dirty old doll that appears to be covered in bruises. What is Mrs. K on!? We troop downstairs and gather back in the living room, round a large but rickety old table covered in a duvet cover, only to discover, as Tor falls through one and gets her bum completely stuck inside the seat frame, that five out of the ten chairs provided are broken.

The laughter is becoming hysterical, but I'm still not seeing the joke. I've dragged a dozen of my best friends to North Norfolk from all over the UK, and we're spending good money on a cottage that should have been condemned years ago, with a living room in which only five of us can sit down at once. But the women have decided they 'love' it! They've decided it's hilariously eccentric and therefore probably perfect for us. Aggs and Vicky have also decided it's time to celebrate with a drink. While Lilly and SJ go back to the car to get the booze in, Aggs,

Vicky and Tor head off to the kitchen to find glasses. Sue thinks it's about time to investigate the oven and make preparations for cooking the monstrous leg of lamb, so she follows them to the kitchen.

Caroline grins and hugs me. "It's really not that bad, hon," she says soothingly. "We're all together and it'll be a laugh whatever happens."

From the kitchen I can hear more giggling, but I'm still in a bad mood.

"I guess… I just feel really guilty about getting everyone out here and choosing such a crappy venue."

"It's not *totally* crappy."

"If I hadn't been so headless I would've come and checked it out properly first."

More noise from the kitchen. A shriek of laughter. Caroline's right. At least the girls are enjoying themselves.

"Don't beat yourself up, everything'll be great."

Yet another shriek of laughter from the kitchen.

"See? Everyone's getting into…"

"Gals!" Tor appears in the doorway, eyes sparkling. "You've got to come and take a look in here".

Screams greet us as we enter. As we tour the kitchen with Sue and Tor as our guides, the laughter becomes uncontrollable: in the kitchen sink, Mrs. K has thoughtfully left us a pile of washing up, sitting in copious quantities of cold, greasy washing up water. Strewn over the dirty worktops are used spoons, dead plants, curdled cat milk in saucers, a bowl of badly sprouting potatoes and another bowl of semi-rotten tomatoes – Caroline's suggestion that Mrs. K has left these as 'gifts' sends us into further paroxysms. Sue continues the tour with filthy cupboards stuffed with enough cans, dry goods and bottles to supply a sizeable nuclear bunker. And then the piece de resistance from Tor: "Check this out…"

She points at a small, yellow post-it on the microwave.

I read it to the company. "Not to be used – for decorative purposes only." More gales of laughter.

"There's another one..." Sue moves to the cooker and reads: "Please DO NOT use gas rings and central heating at the same time. Oven not in working order."

"There goes our lamb supper, then," I groan.

"Unless we fancy turning the heating off and cooking it in a frying pan."

Jayne appears, giggling. She's found the house 'bible' containing information, suggestions and visitor testimonials. She reads one out:

"Thank you so much for our stay in your wonderful home from home. We'll be back!"

"Maybe she advertises in war zones," chuckles Laura.

"Can you find any instructions in there for controlling the heating?" I want to know.

Jayne flips through the pages.

"Can't see any." She stops.

"Here's some instructions... hold on..." she frowns, then reads on:

"In the garden you may well encounter our much loved pet tortoise, Hero."

"Yet another treat in store," I moan.

"He's been giving our family and guests pleasure for many years," Jayne continues, "so we hope you won't forget him when you're making your shopping list, and make sure to feed him a nice, crispy leaf or two of lettuce - fresh only please..."

"She's got a cheek," Laura says.

"That's not all, though," Jayne continues reading: "Hero is unfortunately prone, like many tortoises, to drying out of his shell, so it would be appreciated if you could spare a little olive oil from your dressing to rub on it, every couple of days please."

"What?!"

"She can't organize ten useable chairs, *and* she wants us to *oil her tortoise for her*?!" adds Tor, caught between amusement and incredulity.

"Yeah, right well..." Jayne slams down the bible on the table, looking round at us with a rebel gaze.

"Well what?" I want to know.

"... she can oil her own bloody tortoise!"

Cue laughing 'til you really really wish you could stop. Even months afterwards, 'oil your own bloody tortoise' was a favourite group email subject title.

A couple of hours, several drinks and a bowl of pasta and pesto later, I'm comfortably enveloped in the chatter, warmth and laughter of friends that I've been having fun with since I was twelve, when I experience a massive eureka moment. I realise that I still see and experience these women as teenagers. It's not that I *don't* see the laugh lines or the grey hair or slightly thicker waists – and I'm amazed by the poise, beauty, strength, confidence, warmth and energy of these women, whose lives are written in their smiles – but the girl is right there too, shining through, undiminished by Time – as gorgeous, unique and vital as she was when we were all fifteen. I also realise that the same must be true for me. I'm 50-something, but I'm teenage too, and all the ages in between. I don't *have* to lose or swap the person I was, to be the person I am or will become. Everyone I've *ever* been comes along with me, like a set of Russian dolls. It feels good, wholesome. I dive back into the convo round the table, which is now focusing on a fantasy in which we hunt down, spear and roast Hero in revenge against Mrs. K's evil betrayal. We laugh and laugh. Over the next two days, we laugh so much that when we finally say our farewells it's with happy hearts but extremely painful, pulled stomach muscles.

*

I've written a full and frank letter to Mrs. K, enclosing incriminating photos, and pointing out that many of the problems we eventually uncovered in her cottage are *so* dangerous that if she doesn't get them sorted she's quite likely to end up in court charged with manslaughter. As a result I note that the cottage has been removed from the website, and as of this morning we've got *all* our money back. Result.

So I should be diving headlong back into life and work with the energy of a newborn. I should be doing what I was obsessing about only a matter of a month or so ago and getting on with *doing life justice*. I've arranged to volunteer at my local green charity café once a month (something I've been promising for years now) and I've joined a campaign against the City Council's plan to reorganise traffic in the city centre.

But now that The End has receded back into The Unknown, and I'm no longer a teenager with the giggles, or a new bride with a sun tan, the hot flushes are back, and so is all the mental crap and sense-of-an-ending that goes with them. Yesterday I had some rubbish to take to the local tip. It was a bright day, so we'd cleared out the garden shed to make room for the wood delivery we were expecting and I set off with a full boot, pleased to have achieved something practical in preparation for the winter. En route, I begin to sweat. I've failed to anticipate how warm it will be inside the car so I haven't taken off the fleece jacket I'm wearing and it's only a couple of minutes before I'm really uncomfortable and sticky. I decide I'll have to take the jacket off at the next traffic light, before I drown inside my own car.

I can feel my armpits drenching and my hair sticking to the back of my neck as I slow the car and brake at the next red light, pop my seat belt, unzip the jacket and start to wriggle out of it. But it's small and quite tight and the fleece material's very clingy. As I wrestle, I can't get free of the first arm, and I know I'm running out of time before the lights change and I can see in the mirror that there's a long queue of cars behind me. Shit.

Empty, pointless panic floods through me. I redouble my efforts to fight my way out of the fleece, wailing with frustration as I flail wildly about in the driver's seat, wrestling my jacket like it's The Creature from the Black Lagoon. I cry out as I smash my hand against the side window, then spot a pre-school-age child perched on his seat in the back of the car next to me, mouth turned down, lower lip trembling in alarm, pointing at me as he (I am imagining) urgently requests reassurance from his mother (also staring at me in alarm).

I stop flailing, still half in, half out of the fleece, and try a reassuring smile at him. The little boy's bottom lip-tremble turns into an open-mouthed cry. And now the light's changing to yellow. Shit! I grab my seat belt as the light goes to green, and the little boy and his mother speed quickly away from the mad lady. I avoid looking in my rearview mirror at the driver behind me as I abandon my seat belt, put the car in gear and roll forward. I catch myself in the mirror as I do so. I look like Joan Crawford in *Mommie Dearest.*

Having stopped in a layby to resolve my fleece emergency and put my seatbelt back on, I shed a few tears of frustration. When is this *ever* going to stop? When will I be able to go back to just living, instead of measuring out my existence between hot flushes, panic attacks and days spent hiding under the duvet?

I go for a swim in the hope that I can reset my attitude. As ever, it works some endorphin-based magic. I grab an apple at the café on my way out and jump back on the bus, feeling energized and loose. It's busy with students heading into town for the afternoon so there's standing room only by the time I squeeze inside. A young woman, probably a student, probably under-21, jumps out of her seat next to the luggage rack and offers it to me. Jeez.

The fact that it's a female who assumes I'm feeble and of pensionable age is somehow even more depressing than if it had been a bloke. Blokes are rubbish at judging age, particularly in the opposite sex. Women are generally more observant. And given that I'm wearing age-neutral clothes (jeans, trainers and hoody) and the rosy glow of someone who's smug about having just swum a mile and a half, it feels like a serious indictment of my overall image. I refuse the seat. I wonder if the girl is foreign and therefore more polite and respectful of her elders than our native students, but the thought doesn't really cheer me up.

Back home, S is out so I can't moan to him. Instead, I go upstairs, take off all my clothes, and stand in front of the large mirror in the bedroom so I can take a long, hard, honest all-over look at my naked, unadorned, 50-something self. I've recently bought a magnifying mirror so that when applying makeup I don't inadvertently mascara my eyebrows, but I can't remember the last time I looked *properly* at my whole naked body in a mirror – except that it was definitely long before my eyesight started to fail – so I have to go off and find my glasses before I can continue with the review process. I return to the mirror, vision enhanced. I stare at myself up and down, methodically focusing on each bit of me, with sharp-focus critical gaze.

Wow. Well for a start, there's no denying that arse pertness is only one of a long list of pertnesses that I'm quite obviously in the final stages of losing. My breasts have re-sited themselves, asymmetrically, on an entirely different part of my body than when I last looked. Also, the skin between them is finely crinkled, like silk before you iron it. *Everything* seems to be further down than when I last looked. If I let my arms just hang down, the upper half of them looks like the three-month-old leeks I recently found in the bottom of the vegetable basket. The skin above my knees isn't above any more, it kind of hangs down onto my kneecaps. Even my hips seem to have sagged. The skin of my lower stomach is puckering and the muscles in that area seem to have entirely given up the fight. Ditto my thighs. There used to be muscle there but now it's just Cellulite City. I look down at my hands through my glasses. My knuckles look like elephants' knees and the skin on the back of my hands is papery and semi-transparent. OMG.

I take a breath, lean forward and stare forensically at my face. However many plus points I allow myself for not quite having a full double chin yet, I have to admit that pretty much *everything else* has to be scored in the minus column. My cheeks are covered in little red blotches and veins and they're sinking, exposing my cheekbones, but not in a good way; the sides of my face have grown an even thicker layer of pale downy hair, like an ageing peach; my lips have lost their filling and the flesh around has kind of sunk into the gaps left by the process, so my top lip area actually does remind me of half a cat's bottom; the skin above my eyes is hanging so heavily onto my lids that I appear permanently dopey, and I'm amazed I can *see* out of them at all; the hair either side of my parting is thinning so much that light is hitting my skull through it, *and* I've got a sprout of wiry black hairs growing out of a mole in front of my right ear.

I knew things were only going one way, sure, but I had no idea that in less than a year I'd been chemically reimagined as Mrs. Yoda. I feel previously undiscovered layers of self-delusion peeling off me, like skin off an old onion. Another thought occurs. If I didn't see *this* happening, what else have I missed? Am I already one of those oldsters who can't see how squalid their house has become, or smell the stale urine that everyone else is gagging over?

Still naked, I go upstairs and start sniffing clothes out of the washing basket, relieved to note that I can't smell urine. Then I rush straight back down to the kitchen, turn *all* the lights on, put my glasses back on and minutely check all the surfaces, drawers and cupboards. I don't find mice nests or oozing black goo, or in fact anything more unpleasant than half a dried button mushroom under the cooker. At least I'm not letting *everything* go.

With my clothes back on to shield me from the ghastly truth, and a cup of tea in front of me, I sit at my desk and wonder why life is so unfair. Instead of being given a chance to suck in my guts, and set off on the downslope of life, spotty handkerchief in hand, experiencing the journey at a moderate, balanced pace, it feels like I've been bundled into a stolen-years vehicle and am now being hurtled straight down Death's highway by a homicidal chauffeur. I want to scream: WAIT! STOP! YOU'VE MADE A MISTAKE! I'M NOT READY YET!

I open Safari on my laptop, and in my most desperate search to date, I google: 'I need something amazing to rejuvenate my elderly self.' The first hit reads: 'Amazing Medical Discovery – transfusions of young blood rejuvenate the Elderly.' What!? The article explains that transfusing elderly mice with young mouse blood has had 'semi-magical rejuvenating qualities'. Furthermore, it says the research was done at Stanford and recently presented at a neuroscience conference in New Orleans. Wow! Is this actually possible? Stanford's a top ten US college, isn't it? They're not even total crazies. Maybe that wacky idea I had on the train back from Colchester wasn't so wide of the mark after all…

A knock at the door. I ignore it for a bit – I don't want to see *anyone*, and I'm still enthralled by the magical properties of young blood – but then anxious what-ifs start popping up in my head, so I creep along the hallway and peer through the peephole. Maj is on my doorstep.

"Sorry I'm not dressed, O Queen. Bad everything day."

"Doesn't bother me, darling. Have you got ten minutes for a cuppa? I have something to share."

I put on the kettle while she chats about the much-needed work clothes she's just failed to buy for a forthcoming work trip to Canada. This will be her first face-to-face with one of the co-funders of her latest documentary project, so she needs to make a good impression, she tells me. She won't get down to the substantive sharing, though, until we're settled with our tea. This is another of Maj's very regal attributes. She's conversationally rigorous. I pour her Earl Grey and glance discreetly at her, elegant as ever in shades of brown, trying to guess what I'm about to hear. We sit at the dining room table.

"Okay, what's happening? I'm all ears."

"Well… your hot flushes…"

Oh. I hope the news isn't going to turn out to be the latest bio-fix being peddled on the womens' pages, that Maj wants me to be positive about.

"What about them?" I respond with a long-suffering look.

"I need to ask… do they happen even at night?"

"Absolutely they do." I've probably whined on about this to Maj a hundred times. Maybe she just wasn't listening. I can't blame her, really.

"Well… I think I've started having them".

Wow. I put a hand on hers.

"Oh no!" I say, but what I'm thinking is that this might be the best news I've heard *all year*.

"Do you get the thing where you feel freezing cold all of a sudden afterwards?" she wants to know.

I force my face not to succumb to a massive grin.

"All the time."

"I thought it might just be me," Maj says, obviously relieved.

This is a watershed. At last. I am not alone.

"I'm getting this other feeling too – a nasty fluttering in my chest…"

"Palpitations," I tell her with the authority of an old hand. "Par for the course."

"They're really bothering me, I get them five or six times a day – makes me feel like I can't breathe properly and I have to cough or something to stop it."

"I'm so sorry this is happening to you, Maj," I lie blatantly.

"The sweat thing's horrible, but on top of that, I've been feeling…

not myself… kinda strange… and when I look in the mirror, I just think… God you're old..." She looks glum.

"There'll be good days as well as bad days," I embellish away.

Maj smiles gratefully.

"At least I've got you to talk to about it, hon."

"You bet." This is more than gratifying. "First bit of advice."

"What?" Maj looks up expectantly.

"Mothball that." I tug briskly at the arm of her big, thick woolly boyfriend cardigan. "Any minute now it'll become your worst enemy. Ditto anything else you own made of wool."

Maj looks shocked and not entirely convinced by this, despite me having previously lectured her at length on The Impossibility of Wool.

"But it's going to be ten below in Toronto."

I give her a look that says 'there are even harsher realities to address here, my friend and Queen'.

"If I were you, Maj, I'd go straight back into town and buy a couple of things you can wear over a dress or jeans and shirt that's made exclusively with cotton or silk. In fact, ideally, you need a couple of new outfits with several cotton-only layers that you can take off and put back on easily."

"I do?"

I nod authoritatively. "Any other course of action could jeopardize the outcome of the Toronto trip."

She can see I mean it.

"Okay. Cotton and silk only?"

"Denim's okay too, in certain circumstances. Don't forget layers, though. And keep it loose. That's the key."

"Layers, right. Loose."

"It's a matter of adjusting."

As I say this, I realise that I sound like I'm on top of this whole menopause thing. Maj, on the other hand, looks like she's finding it all very hard to take in. Poor Maj.

She looks up at me from her tea. "I know it sounds pathetic," she goes on, "but I'm feeling a bit fazed and useless. Would you consider coming with me to the shop to help me choose?"

Is this really true? Am I dreaming??? No! Maj has just hopped onto the rollercoaster with me, and we're going shopping. Yay!!!!!!!!!!!!!!!!!!!!!!!!!!

***

POSTSCRIPT - NEW YEAR'S DAY

I'm sitting at my desk. It's my first day back at work after the Christmas break. I'm in my office, looking out of the window into my courtyard garden. I'm watching the ragged band of brother and sister sparrows hopping about in an icy gale, staring at me with their beady little black eyes – and I'm thinking 'screw you, tiny friends, I've got enough of my own problems'. Not really. I'm actually watching them peck voraciously at the birdfeeders that I've managed to remember to fill up with fresh nuts this winter, and I'm imagining them tweeting me thanks in their reedy, ornithological voices, for making the winter's perils a little lighter to bear. And I'm pondering the big question: where am I now with this menopause thing? Exactly how changed, reduced, or mad have I become? Have I got it under control or has it beaten me into a kind of normalised submission?

I guess the answer to that is: all of the above, some of the time. I'm certainly not 'back to normal' but maybe normal was just another stage, or an illusion created by my pre-menopausal self. In any case, my days of waiting, begging and praying for an end to it are over. It's a process, as they say. Or even a journey. The menopause has become what and where I am right now. I've developed 'coping strategies'. And I'm philosophically detached about it, most of the time. Exceptions to this include Christmas morning, when I managed to stick my knee, my hand and quite a lot of my hair to a highly expensive leather gift with superglue (don't ask) and yesterday, when Maj called to let me know that she'd 'solved' all her menopause problems by identifying the perfect therapy: buying herself a secondhand keyboard for Christmas, and renewing her Grade 5 love affair with Gershwin and Brahms. I congratulate and encourage her, but inside, I'm cackling bitchily. I don't want to come across like a bitter and twisted, menopausal old hand, Maj, but let's just see how much help Gershwin is gonna be the next time you're arriving at an airport en route to a job and you realise you've packed your Halloween fancy dress costume instead of your business suit...

***

Printed in Great Britain
by Amazon

57643696R00109